The International
Roadkill Cookbook

The
International
Roadkill Cookbook

B. R. "Buck" Peterson

Illustrations by J. Angus "Sourdough" McLean

Ten Speed Press
Berkeley, California

Disclaimer

In pursuit of the international good life, a roadside shopper may run afoul of local custom or laws. Be advised that Buck and the publisher are not responsible if you are caught short of bail bond money. Just call the nearest United States embassy where caring and understanding policy stewards anxiously await to register any official complaints through officious channels. You might try offering the custody of certain family members as proof your good intentions to return for the trial.

TEN SPEED PRESS
P.O. Box 7123
Berkeley, California 94707

Cover design by Fifth Street Design
Text design by Faith and Folly
Illustrations by J. Angus "Sourdough" McLean

Library of Congress Cataloging in Publication Data
Peterson, B. R.
    [International roadkill cookbook]
    Buck Peterson's international roadkill cookbook.
      p. cm.
    ISBN 0-89815-567-3 :
    1. Cookery—Humor.   I. Title.   II. Title: International roadkill cookbook
    PN6231.C624P4   1994
    641.5'0207—dc20   94-17080
                                          CIP

Printed in the United States of America

1 2 3 4 5 6 7 8 9 — 98 97 96 95 94

Table of Contents

Introduction

Since the introduction of *The Original Roadkill Cookbook*, road travel and fine dining have been properly stirred. Ditch diners everywhere embraced the new challenges of pavement preparations. Now Buck slips behind the wheel of the Buckmobile to guide drivers and their motorized shopping carts overseas. Not to worry, you will be traveling on roads paved by others. The first modern travelers were early missionaries who traveled to exotic locations to take pictures of bare-breasted women for their hometown vicar's collection. The missionaries also sampled the native delicacies and used hollowed out bibles to smuggle animal parts home for rectory aphrodisiacs. After them came a new wave of intrepid adventurers, bounty hunters, and travel writers whose tall tales and travelogues prodded the wealthy armchair crowd to become well-heeled globe-trotters along with their mutant, incestuous families and other hangers-on. Quickly on the heels of *National Geographic* photographers secularizing Third World nudity came a population of voyeurs who could afford cheap air fares, which accelerated the growth of commercial airlines. Then the world political map exploded and borders evaporated. Where it can be found, the Iron Curtain needs ironing. Or welding. Old governments collapsed taking royal and caste privileges (including exclusive game preserves) with them and it didn't take long for the new government officials to discover the American preference for fly and drive packages and, more importantly, the benefits of American hard currency. Any country worth its tourists pays attention to its road systems. New highways and new information highways open up all the formerly closed frontiers and demonstrate how safe and convenient the world really is for the adventurous roadside shopper.

The growth of international travel is in part fueled by the need to discover who we are by learning what we eat. Second and third generations return to the old country to sample traditional meals prepared by those with the time and interest to do it all by hand, and menus that have stood the test and taste of time. The really curious also discover a history of rural roadside dining that deserves new interpretations. This international edition is an exclusive compilation of reports from the world marketplace and shows how tasty the world can be.

As most American roadside shoppers know, roadside menus need not be complicated. A simple *Pavement Melt* needs only a slice of cheese. Almost all of the menu items in this cookbook are entrées. If you are interested in appetizers or desserts, create *Mercezedes* or *Smacklava* from your own Greek recipes. All menus include familiar ingredients. Domestic animals are easy to find overseas and every country has one too many chickens. Wild animals take just a little more effort. Not all countries have a representative recipe but all familiar countries do have helpful roadside shopping instructions.

A significant number of travel guide publishers have warned Buck not to offer this definitive guide to eating cheaply overseas. This indicates *The International Roadkill Cookbook* is a classic in the making, with murmurs of concurrence from international chefs deep down in the galleys. Any number of car manufacturers will most likely make this cookbook part of their overseas delivery program so stock up on extra copies now.

The Dead By The Side Of The Road

Gary Snyder

How did a great Red-tailed Hawk
  Come to lie—all stiff and dry—
    on the shoulder of
      Interstate 5?

Her wings for dance fans

Zak skinned a skunk with a crushed head
  washed the pelt in gas; it hangs,
    tanned, in his tent

Fawn stew on Hallowe'en
  hit by a truck on highway forty-nine
    offer cornmeal by the mouth;
      skin it out.

Log trucks run on fossil fuel

I never saw a Ringtail til I found one on the road:
  case-skinned it with the toenails
    footpads, nose, and whiskers on;
      it soaks in salt and water
        sulphuric acid pickle;

she will be a pouch for magic tools.

The Doe was apparently shot
  lengthwise and through the side—
    shoulder and out the flank
      belly full of blood

Can save the other shoulder maybe,
  if she didn't lie too long—
Pray to their spirits. Ask them to bless us:
  our ancient sisters' trails
    the roads were laid across and kill them:
      night-shining eyes

The dead by the side of the road.

GENERAL SHOPPING AND TRAVEL INFORMATION

Why Did the Chicken Cross the Road?
(To prove to the possum it could be done!)

In addition to looking for food, a drink of water, prospecting a new neighborhood, or going to work at a Kodak photo opportunity site, animals cross the road for the simplest reasons.

Mother Nature requires all her little creatures to be fit. During certain times of the year, animals bulk up and to stay picture perfect, they must exercise. Some climb trees, some fly an extra mile, but quite a few take walks along old foot paths now crossed by asphalt.

On Sundays and national animal holidays, an entire family may take a stroll down to the beach or to a favorite picnic ground. These families skip merrily along paths now crossed by asphalt.

Rudolph knew the shame of not being invited to participate in any reindeer games. Wildlife biologists have documented a series of seemingly simple games that animals and birds play, which include toss the acorn, and hide and go bleat. All involve random running along routes now crossed by asphalt.

In Mom's dog-eat-cat natural world, the pursuing predator and the pursued animal disregard all man-made dangers including yellow-lined asphalt.

In the fall, animals become even more animal-like in their lust for the opposite sex. Hormones roar through the larger male ungulates and competition for the prettiest ladies carries the hoofed animals along lover's lanes now crossed by asphalt.

For all reasons and in all seasons, animals cross the road before their time but just in time for the roadside shopper!

Why Roadshop?

Humans are on the top of the food chain by the power we have invested in our shopping carts and with our road building capabilities, the ability to create a hazardous environment for the animals and a meat market for us.

Most importantly, roadshopping provides foods that are good for you as proven in Buck's analysis and content estimates of the three most popular American entrees:

	OUNCES	CALORIES	FATS (grams)	CHOLESTEROL (mg)
COMMERCIAL BEEF	2.7	500	50	100
ROADKILL DEER	2.7	250	20	10
HOSTESS TWINKIES	2.7	1000	1000	1000

If you are nervous about meat fiber, eat no more than six ounces of road meat or poultry a day as recommended by the American Heart Attack Association. This is no mean feat unless you normally eat only the top half of a good hamburger. The AHAA lobbying group would rather you eat seeds and weeds, shifting the responsibility for good health to an associate group, the American Constipation Institute.

Shopping for and consuming roadkill is exercising an inalienable right. In a recent, albeit hushed, re-reading of documents pertaining to the original Constitution (mixed in with Thomas Jefferson's randy love notes to his slave mistresses) were comments on the "bounte of natur and thee rites of landowners to pursu fox and oter game including blak peopls wit all means of transport."

Roadkill is free. In our overwhelmingly commercial economy, road-purchased animals have no price tag. Of course, bloated insurance companies put a price on the cost of any car damage but your road purchases are free and clear. The attendant costs should not diminish the extra pleasure in being able to purchase a troublesome neighbor's cat or farmyard gander. Your roadside food stand is truly the last free market and all the offerings are proof of nature's bounty.

The Roadkill Sampler

The animal kingdom is a loose collection of furred, feathered, large, and small creatures that call Mother Nature Mom. The kingdom does not include any barely English-speaking two legged animals that call you Mother and other variations on the theme. For the skilled motorist, animals are best viewed as the unfortunate payers of the price of progress and can be tasted as sweetmeats in the bland life of not-so-plenty.

Buck's Roadkill Sampler

ALL NATURAL

The largest mammals in the roadkill sampler are uncommon roadkill victims. It takes the timed and coordinated effort of four Toyota Landcruisers to wobble Dumbo and if the elephant doesn't collapse in the effort, the drivers certainly will. The heavyweight class of mammals includes the top contender for perfect roadside attendance, the common whitetail deer, and other tasty mortal morsels such as elk, moose, and the domesti-

cated musk ox. Large animals are noticeably larger than small animals and able to feed a family of four at a single sitting. They seldom stand on their hind legs or climb trees which is a good thing. Their larger brain holds just more of the same stuff that makes small animals such dolts.

The diminutive field and forest creatures are most often found as cartoon characters or mascots of high school teams. They make high-pitched, feminine sounds and live in holes or dens. When undressed, they look like an underfed baby brother or sister; roasted over an open fire, they can feed an older brother or sister. They can be as large as the fat raccoon eating

4

cat food off your back porch or as small as a field mouse. Few of them can wiggle their ears and very few have any understanding of animal rights.

Ornithologists classify most large birds as birds of prey, soaring high on the thermal air currents

of Zimfar, waiting to drop in for lunch on the earthbound. Large birds include the majestic giant condor feeding on your carrion and the emblematic bald eagle catching and not releasing trout from the best private fly fishing streams.

When large birds run out of easy prey, small birds start to pray. It isn't enough that colorful song birds have to worry about

Juan Valdez slashing and burning their winter homes or Garfield sucking eggs from their summer nests, the warblers must also avoid death from above. Small birds are most vulnerable on runways where they can be puréed by airplane jet turbines or crushed under landing gear during take-off and landing.

Frogs and their warty cousins, the toads and salamanders, are easy skid marks for a roadside shopper, particularly on electrically charged stormy nights.

Fish are difficult to reach with a standard gas-powered land vehicle. The largest fish-like beasts that can be rammed by marine shopping carts are mammals such as dolphins, manatees, and whales. While international law may not be quite clear about your harvest, United States statutes won't allow you to bring the remains home. Most Norwegian-Americans vacationing in the homeland will just leave the minke whale parts in their rental Volvo trunks which have been specially sealed for hauling lutefisk, another horrible export.

Any cold blooded, dry-skinned, or scaly reptile such as an alligator, crocodile, lizard, mother-in-law, snake, or turtle cross roads in the pursuit of happiness and their slow gait is deadly. In different parts of the world, larger crocs are freely given right-of-way or pedestrian body parts are freely taken away.

If the definition of roadkill can properly include any meat source purchased by any part of the automobile, insects collected on the windshield, in the radiator mesh, or by a special bug screen can be used as a quick pick-me-up dry snack or as filler in a meat stew.

The Best Types of Shopping Carts

If you buy or lease a shopping cart, the important choices will be size, ramming weight, trunk carrying capacity, and available accessories of the car. The most familiar choices are listed below.

Subcompacts, called the mini or economy class, average thirteen cubic feet in the trunk which is not large enough to carry a medium-sized animal. Birds and mini-animals will fit.

Sedans, the family compact or intermediate car, comes in two and four door versions and has a trunk big enough to fit the smaller European deer or at least a doe.

Full-sized standard and luxury autos are similar in size but separated by cost. All have spacious trunks to accommodate most animals, certainly those with broken legs. The premium autos, particularly the European Mercedes, have the heft and bumpers to purchase any animal with panache.

Sports cars, fast yet fragile, are not recommended unless there are speed competitions for the finest cuts. Convertibles are verboten because of the overwhelming odds of an animal flipping over the top to join you in the front seat.

Mini-vans or buses are as popular overseas as they are in the United States. The large passenger compartment can be reconfigured to carry a week's worth of shopping. Buck recommends an engine in front (and front wheel drive) to add critical extra pounds of up-front protection and ramming thrust.

Sports utility or station wagons are the serious shopper's cart of choice. With up to sixteen cubic feet of storage space, utility vehicles are also equipped with cartop carnage carriers and four wheel drive to reach the most inaccessible shopping areas.

Recreational vehicles are preferred by those shoppers who require and can afford their own kitchen environment.

Special Vehicles

Bicycles are no longer just a means of transport. In the more civilized countries, the bike lanes that parallel the auto lanes are closest to the road shoulder so bikers can shop first on many

animals. Automobiles are not allowed to cross over the dividing line unless the biker has made an offensive gesture or looks full. In less civilized countries like China, bikes are quite often the only way to do business. In Bejing for example, there are over three million bikes in a city of nine million. The city custom and law is single ridership which raises the obvious question: what are the three million not smelling bicycle seats doing for lunch?

Water born vehicles are not recognized as shopping carts but the ramming power of a fully loaded bass boat is not to be underestimated.

Golf carts are used by smart shoppers who know that the last round of each day collides with the feeding of the wildlife un-

der the care of the sensitive land stewards who built the course. The dead deer tally on the most famous golf links is par for the course and the best kept secret in the sports world, not to mention the loss of migratory waterfowl around the water traps. The carnage is too shameful to mention and a good reason to set an example by carrying your own bags.

Motorcycles are high-risk shopping carts. However, with a side car you have the additional stability of a third wheel carrying compartment. Since motorcycle operators have a high rate of head injuries, throughout  the United States and other overregulated countries, safety helmets are required. In Norway, square helmets can be rented or bought as a souvenir.

Horse or reindeer drawn sleighs are used in northern climates as the traditional way  to reach herd animals. American snowmobiles are the faster way.

 *Trains* are the best for railroad kill with the old locomotives plowing through old habitats. Local unions control who gets the best cuts; a stiff tip to the conductor will assure a fresh choice.

Tricycles are used by children who manifest their base natures by running over anything on the neighborhood sidewalks including angle-worms, ants, and their siblings. The latter is difficult to do on roller skates.

The perfect shopping cart is the Buckmobile, a completely customized all-terrain vehicle. Note the International Red Cross sign which will designate you as an emergency vehicle, which is a handy thing to be. The entire vehicle has been reinforced with armored plate and accessorized to not only carry a full meal deal but to pull one.

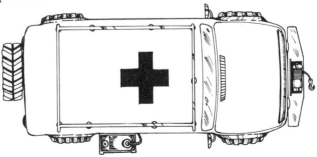

The Best Places to Shop

Wild animals are at home on the range that has a variety of flora and lower order fauna. Flora provides cover for security, food, and comfortable leaves to sleep on; fauna provides other animals to play with and feed on. Each landscape has particular opportunities.

The choices are clear in the big deserts; either shop the easier herd animal that belongs to someone else or expect a high speed chase. Domesticated herd animals such as camels, cattle, goats, horses, and sheep are the sacred property of the nomads or stationary farmers who do not hold to any version of a tourist potlatch. But that doesn't mean there are no opportunities in the great Gobi or Sahara desert. The keepers have to sleep sometime.

Tundra, or the frozen deserts of the polar regions, are home to wild polar bears, musk ox, wolves, and arctic fox, in addition to a variety of marine mammals. Snowmobiles not only bring the shoppers in but the quick-frozen out. Watch for sleeping Eskimos.

If you stacked forest types from north to south, the coniferous or evergreen forests would occupy much of the northern climates, followed south by the deciduous forests, and on to the tropical rain forests where rum is considered a breakfast drink. The northern forests harbor the larger and hardier beasts such as reindeer, elk, moose, and predatory wolves and bears. Familiar critters in the southern forests are boar and deer that stray north or south into other non-tropical forests. Travel near or through these two forests represents the greatest shopping opportunities; many highway departments have laid asphalt right through the living and dining room of all the major animal houses. The selection is unbeatable. Tropical rain forests are always hot, wet, and largely impenetrable with exotic wildlife steaming in the trees. The clearing practice of slash and burn will soon open these markets to the adventurous.

The history of grasslands is one of conflict, wild animals losing habitat to domesticated dolts. Quite often the most stupid wild animals were tamed, like the llamas of the Andes. The others are born stupid, like cattle and sheep. The largest collections of wildlife live on the few remaining great continental grasslands. Giraffes, elephants, rhinos, and hippos can be found strolling the African savannas; antelope, bison, coyote, and deer keep the American west wild. The grasslands are the best testing grounds for the modern all-terrain utility shopping carts.

The most familiar high alpine dwellers are the hoofed daredevils of the ledge, the mountain goat family, and big cats such as the lion, lynx, and snow leopard. Overseas, the high mountain forests of East Africa host the highest primates. The few roads in many mountain environments unfortunately make road shopping almost impossible. Poor winter driving conditions further restrict the opportunities but the few roads that are kept open, such as the ones around Jackson Hole, Wyoming, concentrate the starving deer nicely. The narrow gauge railways that cut through the more remote mountain forests are of little help until snow pushes the animals down onto the tracks.

Other outdoor arenas like zoos, animal parks, and golf courses are useful only as cellblocks waiting for a prison break or shopping exclusives for the occupationally disabled at the ninth hole.

The Signs of a Good Shopping Area

THE ABSOLUTE
BEST SIGN

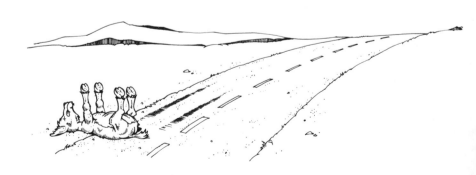

THE NEXT TO BEST
SIGNS

REINDEER
XING

CAMEL
XING

HORSE
XING

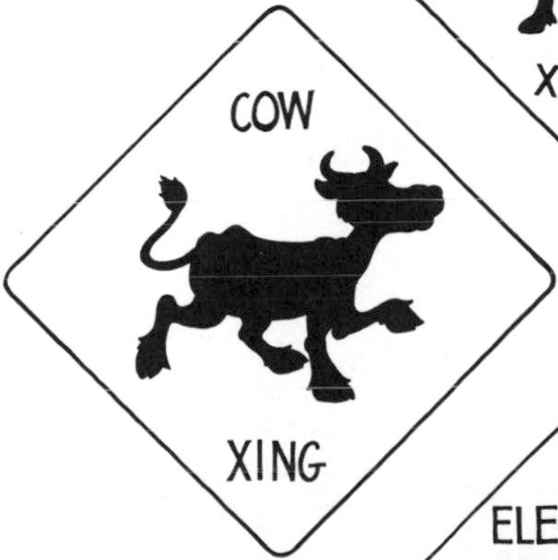

COW
XING

CAT
XING

ELEPHANT
XING

General Roadshopping Instructions

The roadside shopper has two ways to go to the market; either blissfully drive down the bountiful byways and accept any purchase as a special gift, or with purpose and foresight plot travel venues according to menus. The reactive shopper has the advantage of always being surprised; the proactive shopper has the adrenaline rush of a gambler combined with the mathematical certainty of eating well.

Either way, road shopping involves a collision of interests. There are three principal approaches for the driver.

From the front:
Your most important and safest ramming equipment is the bumper backed by the weight of the engine.

From the side:
There are two ways to hit an animal with the side of your cart, either by power turning into the beast with an assist from slippery pavement, or by opening your door to slap the dolt into the celestial wild kingdom.

14

From the rear: Taking a critter with the rear bumper is not impossible with high ratio reverse gears guided by bright backup lights.

Roadside shopping is predictable. If an animal is facing west, it will move west unless something scares or blocks that movement. They do not fake head movements like good basketball players. A bird will most always fly in the direction of its beak. Good sports will beep the horn just before impact to allow a fair wing hit.

The smallest animals and birds may hold motionless in the hope your craft will safely pass over, another reason why thoughtful manufacturers hang the differential so close to the tarmac.

The larger and more obstinate animals will lean into the car, shifting weight off the outside leg to take the punch easier.

The two-legged animals in the other shopping carts on the road are a little less predictable.

When the car in front of you or coming toward you swerves to miss a large animal, the perfect opportunity for a cosmic match is to either keep going straight or swerve into the other lane to complete the purchase. In any court of law in any country, your actions will be perceived as a display of good sense and good driving.

When the car in front of you or coming toward you swerves to ram a large animal, they are very selfish and should be taught a lesson. If, in your experience, you think the car in front will miss the purchase, pass the car on either side and take the animal yourself. If the car in front is aiming well, ram the car so the selfish pigs will hit the animal much too hard, spoiling the foodstuffs for the ugly grouping in their back seat. If the car coming towards you swerves putting you in danger, only your superior driving skills will allow you to choose well.

Uniformed officials do not want you to eat off their buffet lines and have designed a number of artificial barriers to prevent you from shopping. These include fences, underpasses, overpasses, and potholes. Even do-good manufacturers are selling whistles to be mounted on fenders that are supposed to scare the ditch dummies. None of these precautions are effective for the experienced roadside shopper. Ten percent of all shoppers take ninety percent of the sustainable harvest.

The Roadside Coroner

A true sport pays final and last respects to the quarry at time of purchase. In a gesture of humility and thanks for the bounty of the earthbound, a small ceremony can be held along the road or when the undesired parts are buried. Each shopping cart should appoint a designated coroner for the few essential duties:

Pronounce the death and close the eyes of the deceased.

Commit the soul to up yonder.

Bless the food that has been provided.

Prepare the deceased for a proper burial by first removing the edible sections. Generally speaking, the best parts start on the rear side opposite the impact and work forward around to the other side. For those who fancy organ meat, the point and severity of impact will determine whether the liver is intact. You won't know until you open the chest cavity if you really did break the animal's heart. If you hit the animal while it was taking a leak alongside the road, the kidneys may be unrecoverable that close to the ground. But at least they'll be empty. Meats should be washed free of all hair and blood clots. Once you've stripped out the filets, the remains should be buried in some neighbor's yard.

There are two schools of thought on where you should prepare your selection. The survivalists advocate dealing with the foodstuffs at the scene. The camping crowd suggests that the bounty be put into your shopping cart for more private cleaning and eating elsewhere.

If time permits, a quick snack at the scene may appease the loud hungry noises inside the car. Your shopping cart will provide only limited cover while you clean and cook on or below the shoulder of the road.

A deep ditch will provide more cover for your cleaning but no ditch will hide the smoke of your barbeque.

If appetites permit, it's wise to move quickly away from the scene. While you may lose some of the freshness in the temporary delay of transport, you also avoid local regulations, customs, and hungry uniforms. Put your purchase in the trunk. If the trunk is too full of other animal parts, strap the large ungulate upright in the front seat. Officials will assume you are just taking one of the in-laws for a spin.

There are many convenient areas to clean and/or eat enroute.

Roadside parks accommodate the multiple needs of the traveling public with running water, filet tables, and large garbage cans. Fire places or rings are terrific cooking areas.

Full service stations have water and air hoses to wash and dry your road purchase. If you buy at least eight gallons of gas, the carcass strapped to the top can be washed and waxed.

Catholic churches have cleaning cubicles called vestibules which are perfect for dressing a carcass with a holy water fount nearby for wash-up. The votive candles can be used for roasting. Protestant churches are still boring.

You'll need just a few tools to prepare your entrées. A heat source can be as simple as a hot exhaust manifold for quick snacks and fuel as simple as cow or llama chips. Utensils are even easier: a spoon, knife, and fork set, and one pot will cover most cooking needs.

The simplest recipes can be prepared and served at the scene or enroute but experienced road gourmets opt for the more exotic, international world of accommodations in order to prepare the more sophisticated recipes of this cookbook. Gourmands beg off staying with relatives and dismiss the cookie-cutter hotels. They scan the travel sections of major metropolitan newspapers prior to departure, or tourist information kiosks while in country, for accommodations in medieval castles, stately chateaus, or country villas. Unusual housing can be rented nightly, leased, or even swapped with your own humble digs (at a substantial discount, of course). The advantages are many; you'll use well-equipped kitchens with traditional utensils and ingredients to prepare the traditional national dishes. Once inside, the cooking procedures are no more different than your home preparations.

Cooking Techniques

To eat well alongside the road or in the safety of a kitchen, employ tested cooking techniques for healthy dining.

Baking: Oven dry heat is used for the better cuts of meat.

Braising: Brown food for color and closure then cook at a low temperature for a long time in a small amount of liquid. Use a tight lid for tougher cuts.

Broiling: Grill or cook by applying heat to each side of the food.

Poaching: Cook gently in a small amount of a liquid at a temperature below boiling point.

Sautéing: Gently fry in a small amount of butter or oil at a temperature high enough to blanch vegetables.

Steaming: Cook food on an elevated rack using the steam from boiling liquid in a covered pot.

Stir-fry: Quick cook over high heat in small wok with hot oil.

All these techniques are typically used for the better cuts. For those who are used to only eating filets, take a fresh look at the other tasty parts you are missing. A skinned calf head makes a rare in-your-face entrée. Cook the head meat and squeeze into a mold with its own gelatin binding. Slice and serve this heady mix cold. The brains of most young animals are so tender that little cooking is necessary. Soak adult brains in ice, trim the membrane, blood clots, and tumors then blanch or poach. Cheek muscles of larger animals are as tender as the prized halibut cheeks, with the notable exception of herd animals that smile too much.

For a meal that not only looks good but some say tastes good, hardboil a pair of lamb eyes, remove the dark center focus with a sharpened spoon and stuff with a colorful, tasty pâté. Here's looking at you, kid! A nose should be poached or parboiled, then skinned and baked in a casserole. Tongue eaters take their licks in culinary circles yet the meat is lean and tasty.

Trim, soak, then simmer the tongue in salt water full of flavorful vegetables. Once cooked and skinned, it can be ground into a pâté, sliced thin, and served cold. Any foot that has a soft bottom such as a bear paw or camel foot can be eaten by simmering in salty water with vegetables until meat loosens. Remove meat, roll in batter and fry, then reduce stock and use as sauce.

Even tails can be used once shaved to thicken (and stir) rich meat soups. There are many cheesy jokes about the aphrodisiac value of testicles, especially lamb. When questioned, shepherds that mind their flocks by night reply, "Baa humbugger." To eat, remove membrane, season, dip in flour, and fry till brown. Once you've gained an appreciation of other meats, your road purchases will stretch further.

Planning Your Trip

Like most travelers, you have a fixed amount of shopping time so a dining itinerary is important. Using the combined resources of a world atlas and wildlife distribution map, a shopper can leisurely plan a road trip of gourmand proportions. Once you have decided which exotic animals to ram, send a letter to that country's tourist office for road maps and recent motorist information. Armed with this specific detail and a general idea which national dishes you'd like to prepare, you can then decide on exactly where and when to shop. If a mountain goat is the object of your deflection, plan your visit to the Alps in the spring when the roads are open. If you want to time your family migration with a furred family migration in central Africa, your window of opportunity is fixed by their annual movement. Your principal touring tool will be your road map.

Road maps from other countries are similar to state maps, with few exceptions. Major roads in other countries may be called auto-estradas, auto-pistas, auto-routes, or autobahns. They appear as thick unbroken red lines. Green, yellow, or other/no color lines indicate provincial or secondary local routes that offer the best shopping opportunities. Broken lines usually indicate construction. Mileage between cities and attractions is expressed in kilometers which are sort of like miles only shorter.

Road signs with red borders or red interiors deal with major prohibitions. The most recognizable is the big red stop sign. The second is the round or triangle-shaped, red bordered sign with a red diagonal line designating prohibited activity such as NO ENTRY.

Blue and white signs are informational and instructional. A red cross-hatched red-bordered Dutch sign with a delft blue background signifies no parking on that side of the dike unless you promise to buy at least $100 U.S. in tulip bulb seconds.

Green borders highlight permitted activities such as a right turn. Yellow signs with black directional arrows indicate preferred routes.

Orange backgrounds announce road conditions and activities such as road work in progress.

In some foreign countries, it's important to know the hand signals of the traffic policemen. Arms stretched out horizontally mean it's not your turn. Arms stretched up straight over the head mean it's time to go. Arms holding pistolas at you mean it's crying time again and they can see that faraway look in your eyes.

Crossing International Borders

Map symbols for an international boundary are often broken lines separated by dots. Crossings are marked by a road symbol and circle intersecting the boundary. A broken line in the circle indicates the crossing is restricted to local traffic only. A broken body in the circle means the crossing is restricted to the foolhardy only.

Vehicular border crossings are normally open twenty-four hours. Automobile and visitor associations are normally located nearby where they offer services such as currency exchange, maps, insurance, and inexpensive taxidermy. In Europe, border crossings are a major non-event and it's hard to find and convince a border official to stamp your colorless passport. In the third and fourth world, a border crossing is major nonsense that comes with easy-to-find broken toothed border officials ready to stamp not only the passport but the passport holder.

There are two separate sets of uniformed greeters at the border crossings: customs and immigration. Of the officials hugging and kissing you welcome, the customs folk are most interested in what you wish to leave in their country and immigration most interested in whether you wish to leave yourself or any undesirable relative in their country. Of the officials hugging and

kissing you fond farewell, the customs folks are most interested in what you've stolen from their country and immigration who you may have in your trunk. Both sets of greeters are underpaid and any offer of hard currency will either speed your passage or not.

The attitude and clothing of border officials are key indicators of how successful your border crossing will be. Attitude shows up in their facial expressions: if there is a smiling face, quite likely they will be interested in your travel stories and may invite you into the guard shack for a cup of flavored coffee or goat's milk. If there is a frowning face, they may be suffering from gastric distress due to extended home cooking. Any offer of prescription drugs will change the frown into a toothless smile.

If the officials are dressed in native garb, they will be particularly frisky and anxious for you and your square peg family to fit into their round hole culture. Just promise to do as they say, at least until you are out of sight of the gates and out of range of their semiautomatic rifles.

If the officials are dressed in hard, shiny ex-Soviet garments topped with epaulets, swathed with ribbons and sashes, and then girded with hard shiny armaments, they are interested in swapping religious icons and plaster busts of Lenin and Stalin for Levis, cassettes of Elvis and Michael Jackson, and a decent pack of cigarettes.

If the officials are dressed in nondescript generic official garments that could be bought from any good restaurant uniform supply, they are bureaucratic dolts who have a hassle quota for rascals like you. Admit nothing.

Some countries prohibit importing roadkill. If you have chunks of camel remaining from your North African excursions, Dutch officials will make you eat it before you cross into the Netherlands, which will make you too full to eat any Dutch national dishes. Which is a good thing.

Proper Entrance Procedures

Pull to a complete stop.

Beep horn to announce arrival.

Send children in guard shack to use toilets.

Empty ashtrays out of front passenger window.

Beep horn again.

Have spouse change clothes in front seat.

Let dog out for fresh air.

Put hard currency in passport before it is surrendered.

Shake hands of officials.

Proper Exit Procedures

Pull to an almost complete stop.

Beep horn to announce departure.

Pull to a complete stop if gate arm is still down.

Test gate arm with bumper for tensile strength.

Instruct family on emergency evacuation procedures.

Leave transmission in fast gear.

If officials do not appear within thirty seconds, assume they are busy strip-searching other detainees. Proceed on. Even if you have to leave a family member as hostage.

Renting a Shopping Cart

If you do not want to ship your own shopping cart, vehicles can be rented in most civilized and a few uncivilized countries. Many familiar car rental agencies are international and offer the same underpowered cars you find at home. By renting your shopping cart, you can drop it off when you don't want it or can't drive it anymore, and outfit it with special shopping equipment options such as carcass racks.

Decide on rental period: Pre-arranged package plans can be expensive if time allotments are exceeded. An in-country buy or lease might be best. A longer term lease will lower the daily rates. If you buy a car overseas, you will avoid value added taxes and lower any import duties due to shopping damages.

Decide on size of car: Don't be surprised by the models you'll see offered by recognizable automobile manufacturers. No matter who you rent from, you'll encounter funny sounding (and looking) locally produced cars such as Polos, Passats, Destas, Pissants, Familias, and Bongos. Never fear, the major American, European, and Japanese automobile companies build cars from strategically stashed bins of spare parts around the world and these hybrids are guaranteed to take you just short of your destination. It is a very good idea to drive a car similar to the locals. In Poland, over half of the natives drive the Polish Fiat, the lowest priced car that still runs. The other half drive into each other.

Decide on extras: If you have to transport roadkill for any distance, air conditioning avoids excessive spoilage. Power steering allows you to swerve quickly into an animal that has almost made it to roadside safety. Power brakes are handy when you have to slow for a better shot or stop quickly to back over an animal. Automatic transmissions are less bothersome and give you more time to prepare the other occupants of the car for impact.

Decide on mileage options: Calculate the miles needed to fill the larder and be sure the free mileage allowance will cover it.

Decide on extra drivers: A few countries advise hiring a driver which obligates you to pay the driver's meals and hotel expenses. In Seoul, a ten-hour driver service costs as much as W40,000, which is a whole lot of W.

Decide on where you want to go: Some countries such as New Zealand won't allow you to shuttle a rental car between islands. In Australia, a few rental agencies only allow metro use and judging from your appearance is probably a good idea.

International Insurance

Public liability and property damage insurance is compulsory in many foreign lands. Blanket policies purchased at AAA clubs are valid throughout the United Kingdom, Ireland, Turkey, Morocco, Tunisia, a few parts of the former Soviet Republic, and continental Europe except Albania. An International Motor Insurance Card or Green Card is provided with each policy which certifies that the policy conforms with local laws.

Travel accident insurance that covers the occupants of the car can be purchased from your travel club, travel agency, or through credit card companies. A "trip assist" policy can also be purchased to provide for trip cancellation and interruption. An interruption is commonly agreed to imply the hitting of the wrong animal much too hard.

Be aware of the many key insurance coverages and clauses. Your standard auto insurance may not cover exotic shopping carts like Lamborghinies, antiques, or any off-road vehicle with the guts to do the job.

Bodily injury: Protects you if you injure someone while trying to run over their pet or other livestock.

Property damage: Protects you if during the pursuit of a pet or other livestock, you damage another person's property such as a dog house, yard fence, or any previously immovable object.

Personal injury protection: Covers most medical bills if you accidentally ram another shopper while in pursuit of a particularly tasty item, regardless of which driver is at fault. This clause also covers a fixed percentage of income while you are out of work.

Comprehensive: Covers damage to your car other than collision. Some jurists have ruled that a roadkill collision, particularly where an animal has hit you from the side or rammed the rear bumper, is not a coverable collision. The comprehensive clause also pays for damages should an animal fall from a tree and break a windshield.

Collision: Covers all your damages caused by a direct collision. NOTE: The collision damage waiver is not insurance. For a separate fee, the rental agency waives your responsibility for any damages caused by a collision or rollover. This waiver might not cover damage to your tires if punctured by broken bones. The waiver doesn't hold if gross negligence can be proved, whatever gross negligence means.

Uninsured or Underinsured Motorists: There are ne'er-do-wells overseas too, in fact, that's where most of them come from. This clause covers all irresponsible louts from the cultural third world, including members of your in-law's family.

If you hit the wrong animal too hard while driving your rental car and are being followed by lean, hungry uniforms, you can get out of the mess with of the following phrase in the language of the country you are caught in or use the handy Buckster no fault card.

English: There is something wrong with the steering!

Danish: Der er noget i vejen med styretojet!

French: Il y a quelque chose qui ne va pas dans la direction!

German: Es ist etwas nicht in ordnung mit der steuerung!

Italian: Ci dev'essere un guasto nello sterzo!

Japanese: 〔Japanese characters〕

Portuguese: Ha qualouer coisa que nao esta bem na direccao!

Spanish: Hay algo que no marcha bien en el volante!

Swedish: Det ar nagot fel med styranordningen!

STATEMENTO NO FAULTO

Name _____

Address _____

City _____

State _____

Country _____

Signature. VIP Americano _____

I do testify and swear that my steering failed without notice and that I am truly sorry for any damages caused by the crummy rental car. Have a nice day.

High Spirited Roadshopping

Drinking and driving is not recommended in any country unless you are a member of the diplomatic corps or drive a really fast car. Foreign speaking police will force tourists to take breath tests, or agility tests which are difficult to do with a hobnailed boot on your head. Forbidden levels can be as little as two beers. Outside the suds centers of Germany, maximum permissible blood alcohol content is 0.5 per ml. Inside Germany, it's a different story. If you have over 80 mg per 100 ml in Belgium, you can be fined up to 60,000 BF and that is a whole lot of BF.

Like police in the American deep south, arresting officers may be your accuser, judge, baliff, or loving cellmate. At minimum you can lose your driving permit which will cause you to drive even more illegally and be tossed into a jail that doesn't take American Express.

Special Preparations for Traveling Overseas

Immunizations: Roadside shoppers do not need vaccinations for quarantinable diseases if the destination is in North America, the Caribbean, or Europe. However, cholera is a problem in twenty plus countries in Africa, the Pacific, India, Indonesia, Malaysia, and three South American countries. Yellow fever is endemic in eight African and five South American countries and travelers planning trips to the infected areas should be immunized. Inquire at embassies of the countries you plan to visit for any required vaccinations. The shots must be logged on a wallet-sized certificate issued by the World Health Organization. On any shopping trip there is the risk of being bit by a rabid pet or pet owner so prior to departure, have a booster tetanus shot. In the rare event you do get bit, bring the head of either to the local rabies test site for analysis.

Ipecac: If you need to look offended and affected by the violence and carnage of a desirable roadkill, this drug will force you to throw up at the scene like a typical tourist. Ipecac is also useful at large family reunions.

Seasonings: Your favorite spices are usually considered by customs officials as being part of your cooking equipment. Well-seasoned travelers take a double set in case one is lost or confiscated.

Driving Permit: Your local driver's license is good in North America and much of Western Europe. Several countries such as Italy and Austria require a translation of your license to ram. The International Driver's Certificate (IDC) is required by more than fifty foreign governments and recommended elsewhere when officials cannot believe any country would license you to drive and is available from your local automobile club. An Inter-American Driving Permit (IADP) is recognized by most Central and South American countries. If you have none of the above, some countries will issue you a domestic driver's license if you have brought multiple copies of your passport, visa, additional photos, bales of baksheesh (payola), and after a demeaning and invasive physical.

Passport: Apply for your passport early. If you promised to travel with your family but are not real sure it's a good idea, tell them they can buy their passport at the airport.

Roadkill Dependency Certificate: This document can be provided by your doctor.

Road Permits: A few countries require road permits in lieu of tolls. Fines are levied on shoppers caught without permits and shoppers who plan to use major motorways should purchase the coupons at the appropriate consulate or embassy in advance.

Tourist Card: A few countries require a tourist card as if your attire won't be enough to mark you. The card is obtained for a small fee at the appropriate embassy, airline, port of entry, or on the black market outside your hotel.

Visa: Your bank will issue you the most important tourist card. MasterCard is another good card to have. American Express, too.

Last Minute Instructions

Check to make sure spouse kept up payments on insurance policy. If not, drive spouse's car or rental.

Check gas. If you are driving an older Ford Pinto, certain famous maker pickup trucks, or other explosive devices, carry only enough gas to get you to the shopping area.

Check bumpers and bumper guards for any loose parts.

Set your short wave radio/scanner to the police frequencies.

Do a quick check of auto equipment.

Are your headlights working and clean?

Are your wipers in proper working order?

Are your brakes operable or not?

Do a quick check of cooking equipment.

Put children under twelve and other semi-literates in the back seat.

Buckle up. A single lap belt is sufficient while shopping for most small animals. A combination lap/chest belt is recommended for the larger ungulates. Secure the belt and test for quick release. The fastest buckle guarantees the freshest cuts.

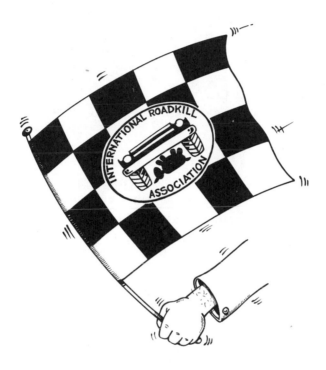

SHOPPERS
Start your engines!

2

THE ROADKILL CUISINE OF NORTH AMERICA

Canada

Our neighbor to the north is the closest major supermarket for the majority of American roadside shoppers. The dining potential in the  great Canadian forests is overwhelming; there are more trophy animals purchased on Alberta highways than in provincial hunting camps. Throughout the more accessible south, roads are in good repair and open for a long summer shopping experience. In the north, alternative all-terrain shopping carts extend the hunting season almost year round. Even the public transports participate in the necessary thinnings of the herd; moose catchers on the trains provide the out-of-control club cars with the following Great White North specialty.

Yukon Smack

Prepare marinade of one cup flat beer (Molson's or any other flat Canadian beer), one crushed clove of garlic, one tablespoon of lemon juice, ½ cup of maple flavored syrup, and salt and pepper to taste.

Soak one bruised bulwinkle butt in marinade for twelve hours or longer, depending on age of butt.

Preheat oven to 350 degrees.

Remove butt from marinade, place in roasting pan, and and bake until tender, basting occasionally with remaining marinade.

Serve on a bed of fresh pine needles with three or more fingers of Yukon Jack.

United States

Regional specialties offer the finest samplings of American road food and each rich culinary tradition blends rural roots with new urban so-phistications. There are at least seven distinct regional dining experiences in the United States and all reflect their homegrown fresh produce and cooking eccentricities.

Pacific Northwest

When the silvered salmon receive the mysterious call to return and die in their river spawning beds, the streams are so clogged with slabs of finned flesh that a high-riding four-wheeled utility shopping cart can acquire a fine Pacific Northwest repast. *Jammin' Salmon* can be quickly cleaned and easily steamed in a wet Eddie Bauer paper shopping bag placed on your hot manifold cover.

California

The puckish executive chef at the trendy roadkill pizzeria, Le Petit Casa Della Yuk in Stockton, is best known for his creative interpretations of California roadkill cuisine.

Pizza with Sun Dried Tomatoes and Leaky Squab

Preheat oven to 350 degrees.

Prepare recipe of pizza dough (enough for one twelve-inch pizza) and press dough into twelve-inch pizza pan. Rub dough with ½ teaspoon Liquid Smoke. Layer dough with ½ cup chopped sun dried tomatoes, one leaky squab that has been plucked, cleaned, deboned, and cut into ½-inch strips, ½ cup chopped marijuana leaves (Humboldt County preferred), and a mixture of ½ cup grated musk ox cheese and two cups of grated Velveeta cheese. Bake until pizza crust is brown and cheese has melted.

The true diversity of California roadkill cooking is expressed within the small non-pizza section of the Yuk menu and is a glimpse into a more pure and playful pantry.

Roast Baby Robin Breast
Stuffed with Vietnamese Potbellied Pig Foreskins
in Sweet Sticky White Sauce

Preheat oven to 325 degrees.

In double boiler, prepare one cup of sweet sticky white sauce.

Flatten four cleaned and deboned baby robin breasts and aggressively season to taste with salt and pepper.

In a skillet, sauté eight potbellied pig foreskins (aftskins are an acceptable substitute) in ½ tablespoon of walnut oil.

Lay two foreskins on top of each prepared robin breast, roll breast, secure with cocktail toothpick, and bake in roasting pan for twenty minutes.

To serve, ladle small quantity of sweet sticky white sauce on preheated plates. Remove cocktail toothpicks from baked robin breasts, slice breasts, and fan slices across each plate.

Southwest

Coyotes are normally a very cautious, suspicious lot except in the trendy Southwest where the desert dogs are fed leftover guacamole from trendy southwest cafes. Once in town, the canines circle trendy day care centers where they run the risk of colliding with the trendy sport utility set on their way to another support group meeting after dropping off the kids.

Mesquite Grilled Leg of Coyote with Peyote Buttons

Prepare grill using mesquite charcoal.

Skin and debone one coyote leg. Smear leg with a mixture of one cup of olive oil, six minced cloves of garlic, one bunch of chopped cilantro, and one tablespoon of black pepper.

Clean one pound of fresh peyote buttons.

Place coyote leg on grill, turn frequently, and cook for ten to fifteen minutes on each side. Remove from grill and allow to rest for ten minutes before slicing.

Scatter peyote buttons on grill and brown. Buttons can be basted with leftover coyote baste.

Serve slices of coyote leg with grilled peyote buttons, iced gold tequila, cilantro pesto, and blue corn chips and tomato salsa.

Midwest

Heartland cuisine is solidly built on meat and potatoes. The great plain states have a strong tradition of comfort food gorge and bloats at big farm picnics, big tailgate parties, and big holiday feasts. The Midwest's renowned red meat is the acme of a cooking culture that takes life medium rare.

Heartland roadkill ranges from king snake to giant snapper turtle, but the most common entrée is venison. Whitetail deer can be taken most anywhere, anytime, and with any size and shape shopping cart. Historically, the red meat animal of choice is the buffalo. The original citizens rammed their more affordable and safer Pinto ponies into the sides of these behemoths to take them down. It wasn't until the arrival of the white man and his loco motives that buffalo appeared on indoor restaurant menus and almost disappeared on the plains. Now the battle for the big horns is on private or reservation property. The politically correct native heartland starch accompanying any wild native meat is the potato.

Scalped Potatoes

Preheat oven to 350 degrees.

Wash four large baking potatoes, then wrap individually in aluminum foil. Place potatoes in oven and bake for thirty minutes or until done.

Remove and unwrap potatoes.

To serve, slice off top of potato with dull knife and season with salt and pepper to taste.

Cajun

The particular nature of bayou cooking as popularized by the famous coonass roadkill chef, Paul Proudbone, is best displayed in a traditional dish that uses everything that can be caught between the headlights. Small animal sweet meats such as squirrel and nutria are mixed with fresh shrimp or crawdads bought from the roadside vendors nearest your skid marks for a signature Creole dish.

Jumbled-Aya

In a large skillet, sauté eight diced slices of bacon and ¼ cup minced onion. Stir in one tablespoon of flour and add one cup of diced tomatoes and ⅓ cup of water. Boil and stir in 2½ cups of cooked white rice, then add two cups of cooked mystery (squirrel or nutria that has been cleaned and deboned) meat and one cup of shelled shrimp. Season with ¼ teaspoon of thyme, Worcestershire sauce, and salt and pepper to taste.

Stir over low heat for fifteen minutes and serve.

Northeast

A traditional beach party menu in the elite enclaves of Martha's Vineyard and the Hamptons utilizes ingredients that can be collected on the drive in from Gotham City.

New England Slam Bake

Line the bottom of a ten gallon boiler with four inches of washed seaweed. Add one quart of water and let boil. When water boils, add six foil-wrapped potatoes and two cleaned and plucked birds (gulls or chickens) cut into parts and wrapped in cheesecloth. Cover boiler and cook on low heat for thirty minutes.

Add two cleaned and skinned rabbits cut into parts, cover, and cook for twenty minutes. Add six shucked foil-wrapped ears of corn and cook for ten minutes, still covered. Add forty cleaned clams and steam until shells open, about five to ten minutes.

Serve with melted butter and your best manners.

Southeast

The coastal southeast is quickly becoming a sprawling metropolis, connected to sprawling resort developments that push animals into easily harvested strike zones. The more sensitive urban and suburban animal populations are slipping into threatened and endangered categories but the rural southeast has not abandoned its easy, relaxed roadkill dining traditions. Even a child with a learner's permit can harvest the marsupial Mom Nature predestined for road stew.

Buck's Three-Eyed Dead-Eyed
Gitya-Up 'N Go Swamp Stew
(Black-Eyed Possum, Black-Eyed Peas,
and Redeye Gravy)

Preheat oven to 325 degrees.

Prepare redeye gravy in a saucepan. Using low heat, mix two tablespoons of drippings (bacon and/or sausage) with two tablespoons of white flour. Whisk until mixture is smooth. Stir in ½ cup of coffee and ½ cup of water. Season with salt and pepper to taste and set aside. Skin and clean possum, then rub coarse salt and

dried red peppers into meat. Stuff possum with one cup of your favorite dressing, one cup of peeled pearl onions, and one cup of chopped and seeded sweet red peppers. Thinly slice ¼ pound of salt pork and lay strips across back of possum. Place possum in roasting pan and bake for twenty minutes or until tender. Remove from oven and let stand. Heat two eight ounce cans of black-eyed peas according to label instructions.

To serve, slice possum and arrange slices on preheated plates with serving of peas and cover with heated redeye gravy. Cover the rest of the bases with a fruit jar filled to the rim with 100 proof Ol' Swamp Gas.

Mexico

Borderline automobile clubs in Texas, New Mexico, and California issue all the necessary customs and immigration forms, collect the administrative fees, and dispense large plastic  bags for Mexican road adventures. Shopping under the new NAFTA accords allows Norte Americanos to participate more freely in culinary commerce. For example, the animals that do poorly in the bullfights are castrated to prevent contamination of the gene pool. The preparation of the jewels as a popular Mexican appetizer is now shared by our new business partners.

Cheese Cajones

Clean, remove the outer membrane, and rinse well six cajones. Cut into ½ inch slices. Dip cajones into a mixture of ½ cup of white flour, ½ tablespoon of coarse salt, and ½ tablespoon of chili powder.

In a saucepan, fry cajones in two tablespoons of olive oil until golden brown. Remove and let drain on paper towel to absorb excess oil.

Preheat oven to 325 degrees.

Mix one cup of grated Monterey Jack cheese with ¼ cup of chopped jalapeño peppers. Place cajones in shallow baking dish, cover with cheese and pepper mixture, and let bake until cheese is melted. Serve with sturdy tortilla chips as an appetizer.

An unusual feature in Mexican roadkill dining is that one shopper has the opportunity to dine on another shopper's chariot: the donkey. A foal is tender enough to be used in pavement pâtés, but the tougher adult needs extra grinding and is better used mixed with other road meats.

Burro-Eatos
(Enchilada Style)

Preheat oven to 350 degrees.

In a large saucepan, heat two tablespoons of olive oil and sauté one chopped medium-size onion with two cloves of minced garlic. Add one pound of ground burro and ⅓ pound of mystery meat (imagination is the key) and brown. Add two teaspoons of chili powder and one teaspoon of cumin. Stir in one cup of tomato sauce and ½ cup of chicken stock. Season with salt and pepper and let simmer. Take eight tortillas (flour or corn) and divide the mixture equally between the tortillas. Fill the centers of the tortillas with grated Mozzarella cheese, roll the tortillas, and place them in a greased baking dish seam side down. Sprinkle rolled tortillas with more grated cheese, place in oven and bake for fifteen minutes.

For a dog-gone, easy-to-prepare snack, the Mexicans have bred hairless dogs that don't need shaving before baking.

Pronto Pups

Preheat oven to 450 degrees.

Skin and clean one full-size Mexican hairless or two Chihuahuas. Brush carcass(es) with melted butter or olive oil and roll in mixture of one cup of flour, ½ teaspoon of chili powder, and salt and pepper to taste.

Spit carcass and roast in oven over a roasting pan. Reduce oven heat to 350 degrees and baste with drippings. Roast until tender, about one hour.

Serve pronto with potatoes and pan gravy made from drippings.

A variation on this recipe is *Mexican Corned Dog*, a Chihuahua dipped in corn flour batter and deep fried.

3

THE ROADKILL CUISINE OF CENTRAL & SOUTH AMERICA AND THE CARIBBEAN

Central America

Central America is the narrow land bridge connecting North and South America and is arguably the most politically unstable road route for the average roadside shopper. The death squads start their day with black coffee thick enough to cut with a machete, if the machete could be pulled free from the neck of a recently disciplined fat gringo. Even international sportsmen stay away from the roads and fly over the guerrilla bands to the hot fly fishing spots of Belize and Costa Rico. The good news about this part of the world is that most personal accident insurance policies will cover visitors in case of accidental death, which can be expected.

Caribbean

All that noise and bother in Central America doesn't mean the friendly shopper must rule out a very pleasant Caribbean roadkill junket. You can choose an island destination as close to the mainland as the Bahamas, Jamaica, Dominican Republic, and Puerto Rico or the smaller leeward islands of the Saints Lucia, Thomas, Maarten, Kitts, and lesser neighbors. To reach most islands, you have to fly to in on a national airline but it's relatively easy to catch an empty boat back to Cuba. Once on the islands, rent a local jitney and relax in the fauna free-for-all that characterizes the laid-back and down lifestyle.

Cuba

Spending money in connection with rec-reational roadkill is prohibited under the United States Trading with the Red Devils  Act. Penalties for scofflaws are up to ten years of roadkill prison food or a fine of $250,000, which is an easy choice for most Cubans.

Jamaica

Nicknamed from the abrupt motions of chickens hanging off the side of the bus or that have been run over by locals delivering rum to  the tourists, *Jerkin' Chicken* is a popular Caribbean dish. Jerk pork and beef are acceptable substitutes, but it's much more difficult to hang a pig or steer off the bus.

Jerkin' Chicken

Combine four chopped shallots, two chopped cloves of garlic, three tablespoons of ginger, ¾ teaspoon of crushed hot chili pepper, one tablespoon of brown sugar, ½ cup of orange

juice, ¼ cup of soy sauce, one tablespoon of allspice, one tablespoon of cracked black pepper, three tablespoons of water, and
¼ cup of chopped cilantro leaves. Mix well and let chill for up to
five days in a covered bowl.

Pluck, clean, and quarter chicken. Marinate chicken in jerk
sauce for one day.

Preheat oven to 350 degrees.

Place chicken in baking dish and bake for thirty minutes,
basting occasionally with remaining sauce as needed, then broil
at medium heat for another thirty minutes or until tender.

Serve jerks at the table.

South America

Shopping opportunities in America's southern neighbor are
enormous and concentrated by land form. The northern half is
covered with the Amazon rain forest, a hot steamy food market
larger than western Europe; unfortunately the road building accompanying the new mining, cattle ranching, and farming pro-
jects isn't extensive enough for leisurely shopping. The
imposing Andes Mountains that form the western border are not
as developed as the high mountains of western Europe so even
Juan Valdez must use his own ass to bring his coffee beans to market. The Pan American Highway that follows the western edge
of the continent is more suited to expeditions and marathon drivers; casual roadside shoppers searching for the friendliest terrain
aim towards the large grassy southern plains.

Argentina

There is no reason to cry for Argentina
with the carnage available on the enormous
fertile grassland called the Pampas. Here beef
cattle are force-fed cellulite collected from ex-

clusive Arizona spas, making for a more tender and slower cow.
Wild game is good sport, particularly the rhea, an ostrich-like bird
as tall as a gaucho and fast enough to require a speed shift into
fifth gear. Once this large flightless critter has had its head
knocked back into the dirt, you can create a sensory experience
common to many on a visit to South America.

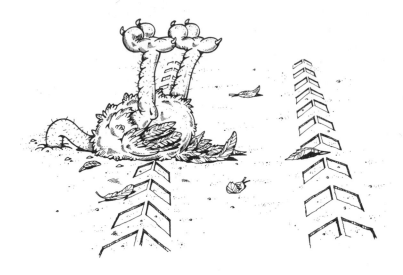

Goner Rhea

Pluck, clean, and quarter one dead rhea.

In a large pot, boil rhea with one clove of garlic, one bay leaf, and ½ teaspoon of tarragon for two weeks or until tender. Remove rhea and let drain.

Preheat oven to broil.

In a heavy casserole dish, melt four tablespoons of butter and braise rhea quarters on all sides. Reduce heat in oven to 350 degrees and bake for thirty minutes.

Serve with a safe smile.

The meat of this bird is very rich and first time eaters could overdose and die of rhea. Those who can bake a flaky crust use the meat in a tasty *Pie o' Rhea*.

Brazil

Brazil is the largest country in South America and contains some of the most inaccessible terrain on the continent. Roadside shopping is concentrated on the fringes of the  great forests and around native villages. *Feijoada* is considered the national dish and this stew pot of broken animal parts welcomes all donations, with the hide used only in exceptional circumstances. Traditionalists use different cuts of pork, especially bacon, dried meat, chunks of beef, and road-pressed mystery meat, all blended preferably with black beans and rice. The magic of this stew is guessing what pig parts are used.

Feijoada Expirada

Soak one pound of black or pinto beans overnight in cold water.

In a large pot, add five cups of pig stock, one pig tail, one blown and cubed pig nose, one boiled and skinned pig tongue, two upper and lower pig lips in a warm and open smile, two pig ears cut lengthwise into ½ inch strips, two thinly sliced pig balls, and 1½ pounds of diced pig breasts. Simmer for two hours or until the smile has been wiped off the lips.

Drain the beans and heat the water, adding enough water to make four quarts and bring to boil. Add beans and simmer covered for one hour, skimming occasionally. In a large sauce-pan, heat two tablespoons of bacon fat and add two crushed dried chili peppers, one clove of peeled and chopped garlic, two large peeled and chopped onions, and one bunch of chopped parsley leaves. Sauté until onions are golden brown, then add one cup of sherry. When the sherry has reduced, add one pound of peeled and chopped pig blood sausage, and two cups of cooked white rice. Cover and simmer for twenty minutes.

Drain the cooked beans and add to saucepan, cooking for another twenty minutes.

To serve, place an amount of beans and rice on a pre-heated plate and arrange pig parts on top in the order in which they were removed from the pig.

Chile

The national dish of Chile, *Chile con Carnage*, has been selected by the South American Epicurean and Economic Alliance as their entry into the International Culinary Olympics.
If you are unable to personally shop this strip loin of a country on the southwestern flanks, this feisty meal can be found in the canned goods section of your local food store.

Chili con Carnage

Ingredients: Animal parts, cleaned if possible; heavily textured and, if possible, hydrologized vegetable protein; wheat flour; spices; saltpeter; cornmeal; tomato paste; dextrose; a tomato's pastie; food starch; citric acid; laundry starch; equal amounts of garlic, onion, and gunpowder; chili flavoring.

Preparation: Pour ingredients into saucepan and stir slowly while heating.

*One serving of Chili con Carnage (with or without beans) will supply the monthly protein requirements of a small Chilean village.

VARIATION: *Chili Dog con Carnage*
Pour above recipe over roadkill dog parts.

*One serving of *Chili Dog con Carnage* (with or without beans) will meet or exceed the annual protein requirements of a large Chilean village.

Colombia

The world's largest collection of large rodents call Cocainia, Colombia's largest province, home. The world's largest four-legged rat, the capybara, weighs up to 100 pounds and properly roasted over an open fire provides a hot roasted meal. In Ecuador, a smaller version, the cuy (coo-ee) or guinea pig is a domesticated animal that weighs up to five pounds and is raised for the table. In French Guinea this same guinea pig is covered with French dressing after roasting. Regardless of size, the rat-like critters are slow-moving targets and can be roasted roadside on a stick like any other small animal.

Peru

With woolly vicuñas now protected, the roadside shopper must turn his or her headlights toward the domesticated llamas standing serenely along the country roads. Locals  dry and salt the meat, then sell it as charqui in the market. For the hungry tourist, a llama can be as good eating as a fat pony. The woolly underachiever is weighty so shoppers are advised to use a fast, heavy American import.

Camero Llamero

Score two pounds of llama steak on both sides and soak in one cup of olive oil, ½ cup of lemon juice, ⅓ cup chopped parsley, and 1 ½ teaspoons of crushed chili pepper for four hours.

Preheat broiler.

Broil steaks on both sides, brushing occasionally with remaining sauce. Broil five minutes on one side, then four minutes on the other.

To serve, cut diagonally across the grain in thin slices.

This popular gaucho recipe can be used on the other mules of the Andes, the domesticated alpacas and the wild guanacos. A capital side dish is lima beans, found canned and mixed with ham in most army and navy stores. Open top of can and heat near an open fire until done.

Throughout much of Central and South America, the chicken is the most vulnerable entrée. There are national variations on *Arroz con Pollo* (chicken with rice), all depending on the availability of local spices and traditions. No-longer free-ranging chicken end up being *Pollo Uraguayeña* or *Venezulaña* but the road shopping poultry dish found everywhere on the continent is *Pollo Rollo*.

Pollo Rollo

Take six boned and skinless chicken breasts and pound them with a cleaver until thin.

In a saucepan, heat two tablespoons of butter and quickly sauté the chicken breasts until no longer pink. Remove and let cool.

Lay one slice of cooked ham on each chicken breast, then sprinkle each with crushed chili peppers, minced onion, minced garlic, and salt and pepper to taste. Roll the chicken breasts and fasten with wooden toothpicks.

Brown the rolled chicken breasts in the saucepan in the remaining butter and pan drippings, reduce heat and cover.

Simmer over low heat until done.

4

THE ROADKILL CUISINE OF THE UNITED KINGDOM AND IRELAND

Great Britain

The cities of Great Britain were once great centers of commerce, full of mercantile activity that outfitted the needs of a far-flung empire.
Tall ships would sail to new and old worlds and return to London with all sorts of booty, including many now-endangered animal species that would be marinated, broiled, thinly sliced, and served up with some kind of brown sauce and called *London Broil.* This cooking technique can be used for any domestic animal, but hungry shoppers leave the barren cities and turn their Vauxhall bangers off the arterials for the more bountiful country roads. These narrow raceways are often lined with hedgerows intended to provide protective fences or enclosures for domesticated herd animals; not to worry, you can still pop a wild pony rooming the moors of the west country or a dormouse poking its head out of the roadside bushes.

Hedgerows are stuffed with indigenous animals including the coypu, imported in 1929 for its fur quality and now ranging freely over the countryside, dragging its foot-long tail behind it. The coypu's palatability is reduced by its rat-like look and the sensitive Brits shower their concern on the more photogenic hedgehog. Intensive farming is pushing the little pincushions out of the hedgerows and onto the narrow paths rural Brits call roads, providing easy marks for those on their way to the ruins at Moreorlesshamptonsteadshire. Over 100,000 hedgehogs give up the ghost each year providing a steady, common source of groceries for animal hospital orderlies.

Bangered and Mashed

Skin, clean, and debone ten banged hedgehogs.

Using a food processor, grind the hedgehogs and mix with one pound of minced lard or back fat. To this mixture add two teaspoons of salt, one teaspoon of black pepper, and ½ teaspoon each of cloves, thyme, and coriander. Grind the mixture again with one cup of minced sweet onions. In a large mixing bowl, combine ½ cup of whipping cream, ⅓ cup of bread crumbs, and two beaten eggs. Add the meat mixture to the bowl and combine all ingredients thoroughly.

Using one-inch wide sausage casings, stuff the mixture into the casings about three quarters full, and twist and tie the filled casings at six-inch intervals.

In a large pot, heat two quarts of water to boiling. Set the filled sausages in a wire basket, then into the boiling water for one minute. Reduce the heat to medium and let them cook for twenty minutes. Remove and drain sausages.

In a large skillet, grill the sausages at medium heat until golden brown. Since the grease will be a problem, deal with it.

Serve bangers with mashed potatoes.

Scotland

The Scots share the rest of Britain's fondness for the hedgehog. But they are internationally famous for their fine beef cattle; red meat connoisseurs tout the regenerative powers of the Aberdeen J. Angus McLean Beef. A traditional Scottish roadkill preparation requires a good beef source and at least one dead bird.

Cockie-Go-Leekie

In a large pot, boil two quarts of water and add one pound of cubed beef (any cut). Simmer for thirty minutes, then add one cleaned, plucked, and deboned chicken cut into cubes. Clean and thinly slice six leeks, discarding the coarse dark green tops. Add leeks to simmering meats with two teaspoons of salt.

Bring pot to a boil and add ½ pound of pitted and chopped prunes. When all meat is tender, stir in ½ cup of heavy cream and serve.

Serving option #1.
Pour broth and meat in bowl.

Serving option #2.
Pour broth only in bowl, serve meat as a side dish.

Serving option #3.
Pour broth in toilet, serve meat to in-laws.

Serving option #4.
With all these prunes, pour broth and meat in toilet to
save the wear and tear on your intestinal system.

The Scots claim *Haggis* (minced sheep heart, liver, and lungs boiled with suet, onions, and oatmeal in a sheep's stomach) as their principal contribution to world cuisine. World cuisine, on the other hand, recognizes single malt whisky as the Scots principal contribution, which is okay with the Scots and goes down much easier than *Haggis*.

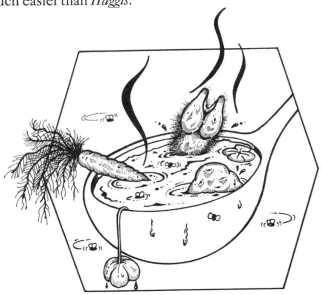

Ireland

On the north coast of Ireland is the town of Bushmills, home of the world's oldest distillery, where you can go down to the malt shop  for a taste or six of your favorite beverage and then cruise south along the east coast, searching the glens of Antrim and Lurigethan Mountain and Tiveragh Hill for a wee roadside snack.

The easiest way for most visitors to participate in Ireland's growing international culinary reputation is to cruise the Eire countryside for free-ranging lamb or the commercial feed lots for the food accompaniment found in all true Irish taverns.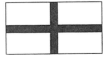

Corned Carnage and Cabbage

In a large pot, boil four quarts of water and add two cups of coarse salt, ½ cup of sugar, two tablespoons of pickling spice, and two teaspoons of saltpeter. Let cool.

Clean, skin, and debone five pounds of mystery meat (could be beef, could be something else). Place meat in a large earthenware pot and pour pickling solution over meat. Drop a weight on the meat to keep it under the solution and cover pot. Soak meat for three weeks, then remove and soak in cold water for one hour.

In a large pot, place meat and cover with boiling water, reducing heat to simmer for five hours or until tender. During the last fifteen minutes of cooking, add cabbage wedges. Remove meat and cabbage and drain well.

Serve hot along with the Irish national flower, the potato.

5

THE ROADKILL CUISINE OF EUROPE

The road systems of Europe are familiar paths for international motorists. The Vienna and Geneva Conventions codified most European traffic rules with three significant exceptions left to the individual countries: speed limits, the permitted amount of blood alcohol in a driver, and pounds of edible roadkill in a driver's possession. Europe is stuffed with bison, boar, moose, ibex, red deer, porridge-eating bears, and the animal whose skin polishes your chariot—the chamois. Europeans are stuffed with themselves and openly welcome any English-speaking travelers as the returning sons and daughters of the American Revolution.

Northern Europe

Iceland

A quarter million Icelanders line the mild coastline warmed by the Gulf Stream and roadshop the 1,400 kilometer Ring Road that skirts the rough interior of the island. Many  roads in the sparsely populated interior are covered with gravel and swerving to smack an animal must be done with care. The roads in the central highlands are impassable until summer and not declared open by the local officials until their home meat lockers are full. Once open, uniformed Icelanders are very specific in their driving instructions: headlights must be turned on at all times to avoid a ryek in the remote areas and driving off-road is forbidden, although the major auto rental agencies feature the best four-wheeled drive adventure-mobiles.

Most rivers in the interior are unbridged and the over forty rivers in the highlands are well marked with instructions on how to cross. Glacial rivers swell with fish late in the day so it is possible to again river bottom roadshop a trophy catch. Fish taken during a crossing can be wrapped in foil and steamed till flaky on your over-heated sport-utility engine.

Norway

Norway is long, mountainous, and narrow minded. One of Europe's most sparsely populated countries, four million Norwegians cling to the south coast for dear city life in win-ter and spend summer in the northern fjords. More than a third of Norway is covered with forests, lakes, and rivers; the traditional consumptive, disruptive industries such as lumbering and mining guarantee a steady source of roadkill.

Roadkill brought back to the cities from weekend excursions creates a meal the average Norwegian can well afjord. Regardless of source, Norwegians seldom eat outside rigidly defined meal periods. Random snacks are not encouraged, particularly for children. Their mania for orderly meals forced the great Norwegian humorist, Henrik Ibsen, to hide his tastiest wild duck snacks in his garret.

Rollunpulse

Preheat oven to 350 degrees.
Split one pork tenderloin lengthwise and pound flat.
Take one large animal (whatever is available) brisket and pound flat. Rub a mixture of one minced onion, one teaspoon of pepper, two teaspoons of salt, and ½ teaspoon of allspice into the brisket. Lay the flattened tenderloin on top of the flattened brisket, roll meats and secure with string.
Add two cups of strong beef stock and eight cups of water to a Dutch oven. Place meat inside oven, cover, and cook

for two hours or until tender. Drain water from Dutch oven, place weight on meat, and chill for eight hours.

Remove string and slice to serve

Sweden

The hard right half of the Scandinavian peninsula, Sweden, is best known for creating the perfect welfare state, with over two thirds of its annual budget spent on cradle to grave

services. Sweden is also known for its high suicide rates aided by chronic alcoholism, abetted by the light deprivation of year-round winters, and caused by the annual introduction of the new Volvo sedans.

Swedish city folks concentrate in the south and drive through woods packed with wildlife to their summer cottages lining the northern glacial lakes. Highway crews place wolf scent along these migration routes to warn moose and other large entrées of road dangers; on the first trip of the spring, smart shoppers place salt blocks on the opposing side of the road. Even with these precautions, student drivers are trained to aim for the rear of the animal which is, of course, a mistake as the rear is residence of the best cuts. Occasionally a bear will wander out of the den and get caught in a side spin and lose the match.

Björn Burger

Prepare a grill. Clean, skin, debone, and remove the fat from one pound of bear meat. Mince bear meat.

In a large bowl, mix one minced onion, one pound of finely ground ham, one egg yolk, and salt and pepper to taste. Add bear meat and mix well, then form into ¾-inch patties.

Grill for five or six minutes each side.

Serve hot with an overhead smash.

Finland

A common misconception about Scandinavians is that most of them are dour, suicidal, humorless closet alcoholics. Scandinavians aren't necessarily dour. In fact, several Scandi-navian humorists are creating international reputations. The Danish pianist, Victor Borge, continues to combine sharp wit with musical virtuosity. A new comedy duo, Finn n' Haddie, are playing the hills and haddocks of Finland and will open the new performing arts hall of Findon, Scotland.

The most productive way to roadshop Finland is to head north out of Helsinki with your winter sleigh. After you drop off your wish list at Santa's workshop just south of the Arctic Circle at Rovaniemi, continue north on one of the two roads to Lapland. For a small fee, brightly colored locals will drive well-aged reindeer in front of your shopping cart.

Donder Up Yonder

Preheat oven to 550 degrees or prepare a grill.

Skin, clean, and lard a five pound roast. Rub roast with garlic and place fat side up on a rack in oven. Reduce heat to 350 degrees and bake 1½ hours.

Serve with gravy made from the drippings and wild rice.

With one sauna for every four persons, steamed roadkill suits a significant number of Finns. To sauna-cook a reindeer roast, place a grill over the heated rocks with a drip pan underneath. Place the meat on the grill and pour small amounts of water over it; when the meat is cooked, add spices and two tablespoons of flour to the drip pan for gravy. While some people enjoying the sauna may object to the cooking odors, others will just assume that you are hosting your in-laws to a seasonal steam.

Denmark

Denmark consists of one large peninsula, three major archipelagos, and almost 500 barely or uninhabitated islands. There are limited roadkill opportunities in this small country 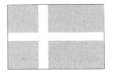 unless you circle one of the many exclusive Danish swine spas during the early morning swine exercise walks. At these tony retreats, the Suidae family goes whole hog, soaking in soothing salt baths before donating their soul and, more importantly, their flesh to the small can industry. Danish ham is the principal meat export of this country and the boned smoked loin is priced to satisfy those living high on the hog elsewhere.

Many Americans associate the Danes with flat, soggy, fruit- or custard-filled pastries; at home the national roadkill breakfast in Denmark is named after an existentialist Danish prince.

Cheese Hamlet

Beat six eggs and add one cup of chopped, cooked Danish ham, ½ cup of grated cheese (Monterey Jack, Swiss, or gouda), and salt and pepper to taste.

In a heated omelet pan, add two tablespoons of olive oil and add mixture. Cook on medium heat until the mixture has set, fold over, and serve.

Danes stuff main entrées and visitors with fruits and vegetables. The offering can be as simple as *Rodkiil* stuffed with rodkaal (red cabbage) or the more formal national roadkill dish, *Rodkildt Svinemørbid.*

Rodkildt Svinemørbid

Preheat oven to 350 degrees.

Split one two pound pork tenderloin lengthwise, rub with butter and garlic, then fill with one cup of stewed apricots or pitted prunes. Roll tenderloin, secure with string, and dredge in one cup of flour. Place tenderloin in greased pan and bake for one hour or until tender. Remove tenderloin from pan and let cool. Add two tablespoons of flour and ¾ cup of water to the drippings and mix well. Transfer drippings and flour mixture to a saucepan and cook slowly to thicken while adding one tablespoon of minced herbs, ¼ teaspoon of lemon rind, and salt and pepper to taste.

Slice the tenderloin and serve with gravy.

In Aalborg, *Kildt Svinemørbid* is served with potatoes; elsewhere, potatoes are put to better use in aquavit, the Danish winter breakfast drink.

Central Europe

France

The French drive like they're in a hurry to stand in line at EuroDisneyland, but their driving history reveals great care for the lowly amphibian. The French chef and national  hero, Auguste Escoffier, was first to admire the well-shaped legs of the frog and dispatched sous chefs during thunderstorms in high-powered Renaults to gather the little croakers for his kitchen. The more politically correct French constructed crapauducts or toad ducts above the roads leading to the site of the 1992 Winter Olympics to save the little greenies. That doesn't mean you can't find the French national roadside snack elsewhere.

Croakedettes

Prepare a velouté sauce by melting two tablespoons of butter in a double boiler. Add two tablespoons of white flour, blend, then slowly add two cups of chicken stock. Stir at low heat until thick, then add one sautéed minced onion, two cloves of sautéed minced garlic, and set aside. Add two cups of cooked minced frog legs to sauce, along with two teaspoons of lemon juice, one teaspoon of Worcestershire sauce, and two teaspoons of curry powder. Return sauce to low heat and stir until it binds. Pour the mixture into a greased baking pan and let cool for two hours. Cut the cooled mixture into 1½ x 2½ squares, dredge them in flour, then bread crumbs, shaking off any excess. Deep fry the squares in fat heated to 365 degrees for two to four minutes. Drain and serve.

Belgium

A tiny kingdom in the heart or, in the minds of its many neighbors, the gallbladder of Europe. The Belgians are considered to be the worst drivers in Europe which may be at-tributed to the over three hundred varieties of Belgian beer available. This also means that your chances (as a newcomer and purposeful roadside shopper) of finding a *Belgian Waffled* are slim.

Holland

The clog-wearing Dutch are known as very careful drivers and the country is rightly proud of the consortium of almost three hun-dred roadside restaurants where they serve low fixed-price three course meals. They do not reveal their meat supply source but their locations near busy arterials might be an indication. Stews are very popular in the Neitherlands; *Hutspot Met Klapstuk*, a road meat and potato stew, is a national favorite. Any animal struck cleanly at a shopping hutspot is a Dutch treat.

Hollandazed Biefstuk

Tenderize with mallet or other weighty object two pounds of bief.

Mix two tablespoons of red wine, ½ teaspoon of black pepper, ¾ teaspoon of salt, with two tablespoons of butter and rub into bief.

In a skillet on medium high heat, turn and sear the bief for ten minutes.

In a double boiler on low heat, melt ½ cup of butter and add 1½ tablespoons of lemon juice, beat in three egg yolks until the mixture thickens, then add one tablespoon of boiling water. Beat in three more tablespoons of water and add ¼ teaspoon of salt and a pinch of cayenne pepper.

Serve sauce at once over bief.

Germany

On October 3, 1990, East and West Germany reunited and six thousand kilometers of toll-free auto raceways called autobahns shared in the joining. There are no speed limits on these super highways unless posted and only the very reckless walk or crawl on these deathtraps, especially along the left-hand lane. Oops, here comes Peter Cottontail, hopping down the autobahn trail.

Hasenpflatten

Clean, skin, and debone one flattened rabbit and cut into small pieces.

In a large pot, mix 2½ cups of water with 2½ cups of apple cider vinegar, ½ cup of brown sugar, one sautéed minced sweet onion, two teaspoons of salt, three sautéed minced cloves of garlic, ½ teaspoon of pepper, two bay leaves, and simmer for one hour. Let cool.

Place the rabbit pieces in a large bowl and pour the cooled marinade over the pieces. Let sit for two days in the refrigerator.

Remove and drain the rabbit pieces, dip in flour, and fry in three tablespoons of bacon fat until golden brown.

Preheat oven to 300 degrees.

In the same skillet the rabbit was fried in, sauté one medium minced onion in two tablespoons of butter.

In a casserole dish, add the sautéed onion, the marinade, and the rabbit pieces. Bring to boil, then cover and put in oven for two hours or until tender.

Serve with dumplings.

The Bavarian party animal of the 1930s and 1940s, Uncle Adolph Skinheadgruber, was a vegetarian who bulked up on cabbage and chocolate cake. This caused his staff and country much grief and also contributed to an abiding international distrust of vegetarians.

Austria

Southwest of the capital of Vienna is a vast, virgin forest and wildlife reserve immortalized by Johann Strauss, noted Austrian composer and accordionist. If you listen  closely to his *Tales From the Vienna Woods Symphony (G'schichtenaus dem Wiener Wald)*, between the first and second bowel movement, behind door number two and third stanza from the right, you'll hear the synchronized screeches of an antique Mercedes creating the national dish.

Wiener Schnitzeled

Skin, clean, and debone dachshund legs. Cut ¼-inch slices on the bias. Dredge slices in one cup of seasoned flour and dip in

bowl of one beaten egg. Press both sides of slices into a shallow
dish of white bread crumbs and shake off any excess.

In a large skillet, melt ½ cup of butter. Sauté slices on low
heat, turning and cooking for ten minutes or until done.

Serve hot with lemon slices.

The tastiest Austrian morsels are the haunches of the famous
Royal Lipizzaner horses. Unfortunately they are reserved for the
bookies and handlers who trip them during practice.

Switzerland

Swiss food is thought to be a composite of
French, German, and Italian influences, but it's
hard to tell. Their national dish, *Rösti*, resembles the
American trucker's breakfast, only more neutral.
They unsuccessfully hide their fondness for roadkill by fonduing
cubed mystery meat in oil, then dip it in mystery sauces.

If the Swiss have passion for anything other than dispos-
able wristwatches, it is for baby beef that has been flattened,
make that pummeled, into pancakes. The calves' temporary fos-
ter homes are undersized holding pens located in tony Swiss
mountain ski resorts, cleverly disguised as the Hauses of Heidi'n
Hans, and attached underground to orthopedic surgical centers
to save both labor and tools. If you knock one of these cordoned
veal into cloud cuckoo clock land, any red meat recipe will do.

Southern Europe

Mediterraneans claim that the combination of a healthy traditional roadkill diet, daily siestas, the opportunity to sleep with a
sibling, and a heavy consumption of cheap red wine all contrib-
ute to fewer heart attacks and colon cancers. Which is probably
true and a good reason to visit the sunshine coasts.

Portugal

Portugal has the highest number of fa-
talities per million registered vehicles in
Europe, caused in part by the parade of pil-
grims to the shrine of Fatima, where three
shepherd kids claimed to have seen the Virgin Mary. The kids,

now adult ex-shepherds, feel particularly blessed that they own the land surrounding the shrine and offer hourly park and pray.

Road shopping for sheep in south and central Portugal is relatively hazard free as long as you don't mess up the nightly count by hitting a black one. Grilled young lamb with a side of ripe mountain cheese, chased with a grape beverage from the nearby island of Madeira, is a roadkill delight. New roadwork in the pig-raising central and north Portugal opens opportunities for yet another national specialty, *Porco de Splata*.

Porco de Splata

Clean, skin, and stomp one large pork filet. In a large bowl, combine ½ cup of olive oil, one minced clover of garlic, two tablespoons of lemon juice, ½ teaspoon of chili pepper, and ½ teaspoon of salt. Mix well and soak filet in marinade for twelve hours. Remove filet and sauté in skillet. Add marinade, cover, and let simmer for one hour.

Serve on a roadbed of rice.

Spain

The Spaniards are slow starters in the morning and stay sluggish until siesta. The saviest and longest living Spanish animals cross the roads in the early afternoon before

any aspiring toreadors wake up. The Spanish shopping cart, the Seat, is just one more version of the Fiat. Properly rigged, this vehicle is great fun in the retired bull feedlots where the traditional rules of the corrida apply; special ramming permits are available to the unsuccessful runners of the bulls at Pamploma. The really unsuccessful runners are accompanied by their loved ones who direct them left and right from the back seat with long-handled picadors.

Olé Molé

Preheat oven to 325 degrees.

In a large pan, heat two tablespoons of olive oil. Dredge one large rump roast in flour, then brown roast on all sides. Remove roast and place in baking pan.

Skin, remove seeds, and chop six chili peppers. Toast and grind one tablespoon of sesame seeds, ½ cup of pine nuts, and ½ cup of almonds. Mix chopped peppers with seeds and nuts in a large pot, and add two tablespoons of olive oil, three chopped tomatoes, one bay leaf, ¼ teaspoon of coriander, three cloves, one teaspoon of cinnamon, and two cups of beef stock. Let simmer for fifteen minutes, then pour over roast. Cover roast and cook for three hours or until tender. Add two ounces of grated unsweetened chocolate to sauce just before serving.

In traditional Catholic Spain, it is customary to reserve a piece of the bull for the church. The Archbishop is blessed with a fine adolescent rump roast; the parish priest accepts a lesser piece. The preparations are similar.

Holé Molé

Preheat oven to 350 degrees.

In a large baking pan, melt ¼ cup of butter and brown three pounds of cleaned and skinned bull tails cut into two-inch pieces. Add six chopped and seeded chili peppers to tails. Toast and grind one tablespoon of sesame seeds, ½ cup of pine nuts, and ½ cup of almonds and add to tails and peppers along with two tablespoons of olive oil, three chopped tomatoes, one bay leaf, ¼ teaspoon of coriander, three cloves, one teaspoon of cinnamon, and two cups of beef stock. Boil, cover, and place in oven for four hours or until tails are tender. Add two ounces of grated unsweetened chocolate to sauce just before serving.

Me molé es su molé.

Italy

Italians take great pride in their culinary traditions and name cities after their finest food exports. The city of Bologna is the home of the famous American cold luncheon meat.  In small neighborhood butcher shops, visitors can sample fine to coarse grain slices or purchase an entire ring of bologna. Street vendors grill ribeye bologna filets to order and serve them on wholy white bread, named Wonderous Bread, baked by Vatican novitiates.

American and Canadian driving licenses are valid in Italy when accompanied by an acceptable translation or a very large monetary unit. Like all foodaholics, Italians are supportive of your road efforts and should your vehicle fail to start with an engine compartment full of feathers, dial 116 and the local automobile club will deliver seasonings, a selection of sauces, and a loaf of garlic bread. Italian chickens are plentiful and form the basis for many regional favorites. Fowl play is accepted behavior whether the village idiots cackle into harm's way or fall off the bus ahead of you.

Chicken Squashatore

Clean, pluck, and cut up one dead chicken. Dredge the chicken pieces in ½ cup of white flour.

In a large skillet, sauté the chicken pieces in ¼ cup of olive oil along with one tablespoon of minced shallots, ¼ cup of tomato paste, ½ cup of white wine, one teaspoon of salt, ½ teaspoon of black pepper, ¾ cup of chicken stock, one cup of sliced mushrooms, a jigger of brandy, ½ teaspoon of basil, and ½ teaspoon of thyme. Cover and simmer for one hour.

Serve with pasta or boiled potatoes.

In Venice, gondoliers bump into sewer rats as they steer along familiar romantic waterways and sing for the touristas necking on the bottom of the boat. Rats swim near the vessels, hoping for a discarded piece of cheese or other souvenir of the honeymoon, and provide the major ingredient for a popular boatkill dish.

Rowing Ratioli

Place a pile of ⅔ cup of white flour on a clean flat surface. Make a well on the top of the flour and drop one egg, one tablespoon of water, ½ teaspoon of salt, and one teaspoon of oil. Mix together with hands and roll dough into a ball. Knead the dough for ten minutes, then set aside for one hour. Roll the dough out very thin on a floured surface. Cut dough into two equal parts and lightly score one sheet of pasta dough with three-inch squares.

Clean, skin, and debone rats, enough for one pound of meat.

Mince rat meat and sauté in ¼ cup of olive oil. Combine cooked meat with one cup of bread crumbs, ¼ cup of chopped parsley leaves, ¼ teaspoon of nutmeg, and salt and pepper to taste.

In the center of the dough squares, drop three tablespoons of rat filling. Put the unscored sheet of pasta over the scored and filled sheet and press down to seal. Using a pie jagger, cut out the individual squares and let sit for an hour. Boil the ratioli in a large pot filled with water or rat stock until al dente.

Serve with grated Parmesan cheese. Pasta doesn't get much better than this.

Greece

Greece is considered to lie within Europe, though it forms the most southern extremity of the Balkan peninsula. The forest roads in Greek national parks provide easy access  to the extremities of the resident fox, wolf, jackal, and wild goat. The easiest shopping is along village roads where sheep and goats provide ingredients for a famous aromatic casserole named more for its dominant odor than the original ingredients.

Mousskaka
(moos-kah-kah)

In a skillet, sauté one medium-sized minced onion in ¼ cup of olive oil. Add two pounds of moose ca-ca (Greek moose may be difficult to find, but keep trying), sheep ca-ca (an easier find), or any edible mystery meat, and brown. Add one cup of tomato sauce, one cup of white wine (not Retsina), and ½ teaspoon black pepper. Simmer for one hour.

Peel two big eggplants and cut into ½-inch slices. Fry slices in ½ cup of olive oil on both sides until brown and drain.

Add one cup of bread crumbs to meat mixture. Prepare white sauce by melting six tablespoons of butter in saucepan. Stir in six tablespoons of white flour, let cook for five minutes, then slowly stir in two cups of milk. Season with salt and pepper to taste. Pour three beaten egg yolks into sauce.

Preheat oven to 350 degrees.

Grease a large baking dish. Place a layer of eggplant slices on the bottom. Cover the eggplant slices with the meat mixture. Cover the meat mixture with the remaining eggplant slices, then cover with white sauce. Cover the white sauce with one cup of grated Parmesan cheese and bake until heated thoroughly. Remove from oven, let cool, cut into squares and serve.

6

THE ROADKILL CUISINE OF EASTERN EUROPE

The Unruly, formerly Soviet, Slavish, Slavic Republics

Since the breakup of the Soviet block, locals who have over-shopped the eastern side of the Iron Curtain are now able to travel along western routes lined with the well-fed four-legged bourgeois. Only poor, hapless Slavs stay at home to compete with the few westerners cruising the wasted urban landscapes of the east. The barren countrysides are still open for road shopping but during the continuing polite debate over public versus private ownership, it's wise to take only the most desirable parts of a headlight harvest and quickly at that.

Czech Republic

Czechoslovakia became a country after
The Big War in 1918. In 1938, Hitler invited the
Czechs to join his rank ranks. Soon after *The Big
War, The Sequel* ended, the Communists rolled
their tanks in for the first partisan roadkill. In 1989, the Velvet
Revolution said thanks but no tanks to the Red roadhogs. Three
years later and still full of national craziness, Czechoslovakia split
into two states, the Czech and Slovak Republics. The former
contains two of the three original provinces, Bohemia and

Moravia, while the latter encompasses the third, Slovakia. The two major cultural groups are the Slovaks who speak Slovak and the Czechs who speak Czech. The Bohemians speak Gibberish and are the major Caucasian ethnic group of Berkeley, California.

An essential stop in the new Czech state is the city of Budejovice (or Budweis in Old German), the original home of the American roadside shopper's cold carbonated beverage of choice. Tours of the original brewery are accomplished by great stealth on dark nights.

The capital cities of Prague and Bratislava are where you'll most likely stand trial for any unexplained road adventure. The noted Austrian-Czech humorist, Franz Kafka, wrote a very funny book about trials which is an excellent primer for those who czech out the wrong animal. As you motor through the countryside, whizzing by red-tiled village houses, a stray farm pig may be fooled by your oinks and become the principal ingredient in the national dish named after a folk hero and traditionally served on New Year's Eve.

Alexander Duped 'n Czeched
Veprovy Ovar S Křenem

Singe facial hair from one pig's head. Remove tongue and eyeballs and close eyelids. Place head in large pot with enough cold water to cover, heat to simmering and add one chopped onion, two chopped carrots, ½ cup of chopped celery root, three peppercorns, ½ teaspoon of allspice, and one bay leaf. Let simmer until face begins to fall off.

Serve hot with pasta and sliced lemons to your favorite mustachioed playwright.

Georgia

In the days of the Tsar, the masters of the manse practiced the traditional Georgian landowner sport of peasant hunting, a variety of not-necessarily feathered upland game. Peasants taken during the fall drive would be drawn and quartered, with grieving families each receiving one large potato for their loss. After the breakdown of Communist control, new landowners invited the peasants to embrace the traditions of the past, with little response.

Germany (East)

Before reunification, East German *hausfraus* queued up daily for the chance to buy bruised turnips while their hausmeisters operated heavy equipment under the influence of heavy intoxicants in their toxic industrial plants. Their more prosperous and thoughtful western relatives saved roadkill bones to smuggle east in gunny sacks. Most of the sacks passed border guard inspection as just more cold war casualties.

Knocked Knochen

In a large pot, heat ¼ cup of fat and brown three pounds or two feet of shin bone. Add two cups of seasoned (basil, tarragon, thyme) stock and ½ cup of unseasoned stock. To the stock and shin bone add one bay leaf, two cloves of minced garlic, two sprigs of fresh thyme, ¼ teaspoon of pepper, and three chopped carrots. Stir in one tablespoon of flour, then add ⅓ cup of white wine. Cover and simmer for two hours.

For better or wurst, serve knochen by placing bone on platter, cover bone with gravy, and top with cooked carrots.

Hungary

Visiting motorists start their vacation in Budapest, the Paris of Eastern Europe, on the great River Danube. Over two of ten million Hungarians live in the capital, a city of actually  three cities, Obuda, Buda, and Pest (the latter the ancestral home of most mothers-in-law). Roads branch out from Budapest and Hungarians are not legally allowed to drive the arterials drunk. There are four stages of Hungarian drinking: after the first gallon a native son grows cheery; after the second, melancholic; after the third, bullish; and after the fourth, sleepy and asking for the keys to the horsedrawn Soviet-made cars.

Hungarian cuisine has an old reputation for being hot. When the Turks marched through Hungary, they brought the little Oriental pepper, especially those paprikas that are mild and sweet. Now the spice is found in any form of *gulyas* (goulash). Meat stews are as varied as available ingredients and fresh roadkill provides for the best of Hungary man stews.

Hungarian Gruelash

Clean, skin, and cut into cubes two pounds of mystery meat. In a large pot, heat ¼ cup of olive oil and brown meat on all sides. Add four chopped onions, one minced clove of garlic, three seeded and julienned sweet green peppers, and one chopped large tomato. Add three cups of water and two teaspoons of paprika and bring to boil. Reduce heat to simmer and add three peeled and cubed potatoes. Cover and simmer for two hours.

On Halloween, *Hungarian Ghoulash* is often served with a rich, red wine called Bull's Blood. But Tokay is okay!

Poland

Poland is unfairly not so well-known for
its variety of landscapes, especially its great
forests and marshes. The Bialowieska National Park, encompassing much of the Great
Bialowieska Forest, is home to free-ranging humped European
bison; unfortunately the only vehicle access is by supervised
horsedrawn carts along circular park routes. With this oppressive
monitoring, the best souvenir of a trip to the forest is the bison
grass which gives the special color and flavor to Zubrowka, the
popular Polish vodka. The largest marsh in central Europe is the
Biebrza Marsh in northeast Poland, but the only easy access is by
boat during the spring floods. But then again, an animal isolated
by high waters might be willing to be rescued. Or almost rescued.

Polish roads are admittedly in sad need of repair, particularly those running north to south linking Scandinavia with the
Mediterranean basin, and those east to west, from Moscow to
Berlin. It's probably best to stay on the rural roads full of wagons
carrying agricultural products to and fro. If you hit a horse, custom dictates that you pay fair black market value for the produce
and provide an Ace bandage for the driver.

Every country has its own national stew. In Poland, *Bigos* is
the end-of-shopping following a full day of bumping through the
natural resources.

KaPOWski
(Hunter's Stew)

Soak one cup of sliced mushrooms in hot water for thirty minutes. Drain, set aside, and reserve water.

In a large skillet, heat ¼ cup of olive oil and sauté two pounds of mystery meat cut into cubes, ¼ pound of sliced garlic sausage, one large chopped onion, sliced mushrooms, and two chopped slices of bacon. Remove meats and add two tablespoons of flour to the drippings on low heat. Stir and slowly add one cup of red wine and ¾ cup of mushroom water. Return meats to skillet and add 2½ pounds of sauerkraut, four tablespoons of chopped parsley leaves, two tablespoons of sugar, and ½ teaspoon each of salt and pepper. Cover and simmer for one hour.

Lift lid from skillet and smell. If stew smells as bad as it sounds, open one gallon of Polish vodka. When consciousness returns, reheat stew.

Serve with boiled potatoes.

Russia

The motherland has a distinguished history of extinguished road food and the traditions are easily traced through their great literary works. *The Song of Igor's Campaign* is considered the first road book, a twelfth century "literary masterpiece" according to Vladimir Nabokov (famous butterfly and adolescent schoolgirl collector), which traces the steppes of four territorial princes on a military-style shopping expedition. The traditions of road memoirs didn't reach full bloom, however, until the nineteenth century publication of the two roadkill classics by Leo Tolstoy; *War and Piece*, an exhaustive description of an unsuccessful French shopping expedition into the Russian heartland, and *Anna Careenina*, a pioneering work sympathetic to the needs of a Russian woman to drive her own shopping cart. The spirited travelogues disappeared when the Imperial shopping carts were collectivized by Bolshevik bullies in 1917 and Soviet apparatchik artists parroted party lines from yawning heights. When Pushkin came to shove, the "new" Soviet Boris just wasn't Godunov.

Though most politicos in the 1920's were outwardly against any signs of revisionist epicureanism, Leon Trotsky gave up his powerful position as member of the Bolshevik central committee and founder of the Red Army and moved to Mexico in search of the perfect molé sauce. Josef Stalin encouraged him and sent Trotsky an ice ax by OGPU courier to help him climb into the high mountain vil-

lages that were rumored to hold the sauce of his dreams. Trotsky died unfulfilled, but optimistic. His last words were, "Beats getting snowed on in a gulag."

The most familiar Russian road dish is an entrée soup, spring beet root soup. By the time the few cow parsnips and other vegetables from the collective farm have been picked over by the remaining low level bureaucrats, the remaining bottom-of-the-cart or on-the-road ingredients have been thoroughly prepared for *Squorscht.*

Squorscht

In a large pot, cover one crushed carrot, one crushed large onion, and two crushed beets with boiling water. Cover and simmer for twenty minutes. Add one tablespoon of butter, two cups of mystery meat broth or water, one tablespoon of vinegar, and ¼ head of squashed cabbage. Simmer for 15 minutes.

Serve soup in individual bowls and top each with one tablespoon of soured cream.

Squorscht is a popular dish at the summer resorts in the White Russian Mountains, pleasure palaces collectively grouped as the Squorscht Belt. One of the many features of the Belt is nightly live entertainment starring former Soviet dancing bears.

Ukraine

Ukranian culinary reputation rests on their incredible, inedible gaily decorated eggs, served by incredible, inedible gaily decorated native women. The eggs

come from Tiffany Nouveau chickens who lay only one egg a year due to the difficulty in passing the ornate egg. Chickens who do not lay at least one egg a year are cut into serving portions, dusted with flower, rolled in egg mixture, browned, baked, then covered in the last minutes with yogurt.

Former Yugoslavia

Former Yugoslavia is known as the European prune capital. The native plum is dried, then eaten stewed or with other dried fruit. Even the native brandy, Slivovitsa, is made from prunes and regular use keeps the nation drunk, yet regular.

Not known for its political stability, the six republics that make up Yugoslavia are fighting over the national driving regulation that prohibits children under twelve and other intoxicated persons from riding in the front seat. The in-fighting has kept many Slavs at home. Even on the aptly named Highway of Brotherhood and Unity between Belgrade and Zegred, you'll note greatly reduced traffic forty miles out of Zegred and hawks circling the grassy verges for damaged feral cats. What with all the lowland uncertainties, head over the western mountains for a chance to pop a brown bear or deer on the way to the beaches on the Adriatic coast, unless you've rented the national automobile, the Yugo. Which means you don't go.

Miscellaneous

The small countries of Byelorussia, Estonia, Anemia, Latvia, and Lithuania are known for their fiercely obscure cuisine and independent nature, with the exception of Anemia which noticeably lacks vigor and vitality.

7

THE ROADKILL CUISINE OF AFRICA

Still the dark continent for a few white European malcontents, Africa is properly divided into the Arabic Far North, the Black Central and South, with the small white jockstrap of South Africa covering the Cape of the Last Great White Hope. Except for the notable exception of the Atlas Mountains capping the north west shoulder, North Africa is dominated by the Sahara, a mammoth dry, empty space that stretches from the Atlantic to the Red Sea. This thousand-mile wide desert is thinly populated by nomadic Bedouins, Berbers, and Tuaregs and their herds of sheep, goats, and one-humped dromedaries. North Central Africa is topped with a large, grassy plain called the Sudan, sitting above the largely impenetrable tropical rain forest of the Congo Basin of west Africa. The savannas are alive with herds of giraffes, wildebeests, and zebras with only the cheetah and the lion, er, make that the lioness as competition. East Africa's large grassy plateaus east of Lakes Tanganyika and Nyasa are packed with elephants and rhinos, making up for the dust and drought bowl of west Africa and the Kalahari Desert of South Africa.

Roadkill opportunities in Africa are remarkable and predictable; fine dining accompanies the crossing of any domestic or wild herd migration. Informal roadkill partnerships are already in place with local farmers that interrupt migrations with fences for their herd animals. Guide service can be purchased from the famous roadkill natives, the Youbangis, a small sect of the Sara tribe in central Africa whose women distinguish their looks with pierced lips stretched around small Land Rover hubcaps. Road-kill food selections from the African bazaar resemble a domestic safariland, yet each unusual species present unusual shopping conditions.

Cheetah: Able to run as fast as sixty miles per hour, few rental cars or full guide services can keep up with both the speed and quick turns of these cat food burglars. Best to shop cheetahs while they are feeding on carrion that really belongs to you.

Elephant: As captured in the early Disney documentaries, elephants fly over much of central Africa. The occasional midair collisions reinforce the native and touring shoppers belief that the gods really are crazy.

Dumbo Gumbo

Clean, skin, and cut into manageable pieces one elephant part. Dredge the pieces in flour.

In a large pot, heat ¼ cup of bacon drippings and brown the meat. Add four cups of water and simmer until meat is tender. Remove bones. Add three chopped tomatoes, one cup of corn niblets, two cloves of minced sautéed garlic, one large minced sautéed onion, two large seeded and cubed green peppers, one cup of sliced okra, ½ teaspoon of salt, ½ cup of uncooked rice, and five cups of water.

Simmer uncovered for thirty minutes, then add two teaspoons of filé powder, stir well, and serve to the sveld barbarians.

Gazelle: Once Hollywood discovered Africa in the forties and fifties, safari tents along Beverly Hill's Rodeo Drive emptied for a chance to sleep in a foreign bush. The savanna stages were crowded with entertainers of all affectations and white hunters rammed overtime to provide fresh roadkill to those singing for their supper. One particular backlot bwana buffet centered around the large rump roast of a common herd animal with the intelligence of a taro root. *Gazelle Mackenzie* was and is on everyone's culinary hit parade. Gazelles continue to be an easy hit in the parade of the African herd animals.

Giraffe: Arabs have hunted the tallest living four-legged herbivore for centuries. Not too tasty unless you pop a young one, giraffe meat usually ends up as *biltong*, lean strips of meat dried in the open air. Giraffes have a shorter memory than elephants and are not generally disturbed by humans and their road noises. At night they become a genuine road hazard with eyes too high to reflect headlights. During the day, a giraffe may run alongside the car and, without warning, cross and block your path. Their legs are long and hard and shoppers concentrate on cracking or "smoking" the shin bones.

Marrow Burrowed

Preheat oven to 300 degrees.

Skin and clean one giraffe leg, then cut bone into two-inch pieces. Dip the pieces in olive oil, then dredge in flour. In a saucepan, heat ¼ cup of olive oil and brown the pieces. Remove the pieces and place them in a baking pan, add enough seasoned stock to cover lower half of bones, cover, and bake for 1½ hours.

Serve marrow as is, or remove from bone and serve on crackers, or remove marrow, roll in batter, and deep fry.

Hippo: A "river horse" can feed a bus load of hungry tourists. Shopping is best done when they feed on grasses during the cooler African nights. If rammed properly, a combo meal can be acquired with a brace of oxpecker birds that eat insects on the hippo. If improperly rammed, call AAAfrica for roadside assistance.

Hyena: Even in hungriest Africa, there is a general resistance to eating wild dog. That doesn't mean a casual shopper should avoid a purchase. Skills learned in dropping a wild dog can be used at home. Hyenas are carnivores that feed on easy carrion and, in an actively shopped area, the hyena that laughs last shouldn't.

Lion: If you want to beard the lion in his den, mark any dead carcass then accelerate your rat patrol shopping cart through the adjacent tall grass for the mane man sleeping off a food hangover. The male lion, whose tail has been twisted off and courage removed, is the national emblem of Great Britain, the Mouse That Roared. In a strange twist of fate, the female or lioness is the provider and a lion with no pride is called a loner (or loser). All the great cat cuts, such as lion loin, taste much better than their distant dwarf domestic relatives who eat boatkill dolphin. All are prepared in a similar fashion.

Rhinoceros: There is no good reason to roadshop an armored animal with an attitude.

Wildebeest: This common wild herd animal presents the greatest shopping opportunity during its lengthy migrations. For shoppers who watch the Discovery Channel, this information is nothing gnu. Crocodiles take their allotments at the river's edge but there are plenty of smarter wildebeest left over. All can be prepared as any large red meat animal, except maybe cooked a little longer.

Zebra: Sausage made from zebra meat is a cultural curiosity and the lean horse meat is usually mixed with pork or lamb. The prime cuts can be prepared as any other rodeo animal. It is wise to avoid taking an older male zebra during the rut; in addition its meat being flavored by hormones, the horny male becomes very agitated when removed from the play pen.

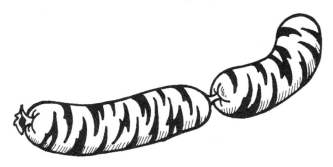

In the just released *Private Papers of Tarzan*, edited by Sir David Hind Parts, the jungle world of central Africa is portrayed as being less harmonious than first suggested. Jane was a social lioness who required expanding quantities of exotic foodstuffs for her tree top dinner parties, forcing her mate to violate many of the sacred oaths he had made with his menagerie. In the footnotes there are oblique references to *Cheetah Cheetoes* served on a burrow of edgar rice, not to mention unusual black and white photos of Boy with an international pop star.

White South Africa

South Africa

With the Dutch as original agriculturalists, the roadkill cuisine of the last large white settlement in Africa unfortunately reflects the nationality of the settler. The great tribes, the Zulus and Kaffirs, still occupy the remote territories rich with wildlife and are much closer to a good meal deal than the original conquerors. Their citified cousins who left the good life to work in deep shaft diamond mines, cruise the white bossman parking lots to assemble the ingredients of a forbidden native rhode kill dish.

DeBoer Apartfried

Skin and clean one boer, then cut into pieces. Dredge pieces in white flour.

In a large skillet, heat several cups of olive oil.

Fry the pieces in the olive oil until golden brown, remove and drain.

Serve with pan gravy and freshly cut carets.

8

THE ROADKILL CUISINE OF THE MIDDLE EAST

Located midway between the Near East and the Far East and often called Southwest Asia, this region stretches as far west as Libya in Africa and east to Afghanistan. The predominate Moslem faith forbids eating of pork, so chicken dominates the domestic meat selections in both public and private places. Eggplant is the omnipresent side dish and is served puréed like mashed potatoes, boiled with garlic, paprika, and green pepper, or fried in olive oil and stuffed with cheese. Each country has national variations on the same theme and most of the border disputes have been found to be cover-ups for long-standing food feuds. Should the Jordanians be or not be allowed to add peanuts to the cheese stuffing?

Egypt

Egypt is in the northeast corner of Africa and almost all Egyptians live in and around the port cities along the fertile north and east coast. In the historically important Nile River delta,  the majority live in villages near one of the most popular tourist sites: the homes of Ramses I, II, and III, the latter best known for its ribbed design for maximum stimulation. It's like a thousand tiny fingers urging a subject to let go.

Automobile importation and rental is complicated in Egypt. To enter the Sinai, cars must be gas operated, driven by a

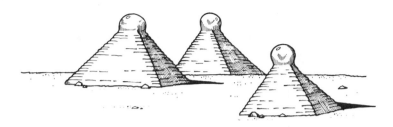

driver with a special visa, and able to pass through the eye of a needle. Four-wheel drive vehicles must have prior entry approval and be on call for the ministry of defense, particularly those utility vehicles that work.

It's commonly thought that all Egyptians feast off groaning tables of exotic foods under the shade of palm trees, but farmers across north Africa often settle for a bowl of thick mush steamed over meat broth. *Couscous* (or in Turkey *Kiskis Kuskus*) uses the grain of the wheat left behind once the flour has been sifted and takes on the taste of any meat cooking alongside the road.

No ExCouscous

In a stewpot, bring three cups of stock to a boil and add two pounds of cubed mystery meat (lamb or whatever else is loose), two large sliced turnips, three large sliced carrots, one large chopped onion, ½ teaspoon of salt and ¼ teaspoon of pepper. Reduce heat and simmer for thirty minutes, then add two large sliced zucchinis, two large chopped tomatoes, one small chopped cabbage, and ¼ cup chopped parsley leaves. Simmer for another thirty minutes.

Fit a gauze blanket lined colander over the stewpot and place one pound of semolina inside. Let simmer for thirty minutes. Remove and turn semolina into a bowl, sprinkle with cold water, and stir. Return semolina to colander for an additional thirty minutes.

Serve by making a small mound of the cooked semolina on each plate, then covering the mound with the meat and vegetables.

Iran, Iraq and Kuwait are on the western side of the subcontinent where Americans test the latest in military hardware. It's rare to find local civilian roadkill shoppers in these burnt parts of Southwest Asia, but expeditionary forces report dining opportunities wherever advance patrols cross traditional shepherd routes.

Iran

Herds of sheep and their keepers are common sights on the outskirts of Iranian cities, even more common near the villages. Fresh lamb figures prominently in all Iranian dishes and their roast lamb is stuffed with so much rice and raisins that the pastry cart is ignored. A side of pistachios, the national aphrodisiac, has the Persians curling up on their rugs for dessert.

Anything skewered on a bumper in the once proud home of Omar and his not quite alright brother, Homer Khayyam, is called a *kebab* (or *kabob*). This national Iranian dish assures the silence of the lambs.

Shushed Kebabs

Prepare a grill.

Skin, clean, and debone two pounds of lamb, then cut into two-inch cubes. Thickly slice two large tomatoes, two large onions, and one large seeded green pepper.

In a mixing bowl, prepare a marinade of one cup olive oil, ¾ teaspoon of salt, and ¼ teaspoon of pepper. Add the meat and vegetables and let stand for two hours, then drain and reserve the marinade.

Take three skewers and thread the meat and vegetables, alternating the meat with the vegetables. Grill the skewers until browned, basting with the marinade.

Serve on a bed of rice facing Mecca.

Iraq

The most recent Iraq entry to international cuisine is the *Kurd Kebab*. Available only in remote mountain settings, *Kurd Kebabs* are served up with small helpings of air-dropped rice, no whey.

Kuwait

During Operation Desert Storm, members of Uncle Sam's expeditionary forces motored with vehicles especially equipped for military shopping. As one Buckster sergeant so accurately put it, camels "are very large and . . . can really mess up some of the Japanese import trucks. Camels can be found wandering in the road, day or night and make no attempt to get out of the way. If you can't find one on the road, just head out for the desert. They're everywhere. Once you've made your purchase, you should get it and go as the selling price is on line with a good used car. If you're in the desert and no Bedouins are around, take your time."

The good sergeant's recipe was to stuff 150 boiled eggs into fifty pounds of tomatoes, which were then stuffed into twenty roasted chickens, which were then stuffed into four lambs, which were finally stuffed into the camel and roasted until tender or until the hump explodes. Good advice from one of our fighting best.

Israel

Pilgrimages to the holy sites in Bethlehem, Jerusalem, Nazareth, and Galilee creates road problems; first time visitors may prefer the safety of pre-arranged shopping. Reservations for the sheruts, the shared cabs connecting a few destinations, should be made in advance. Most public transportation is available on short notice. A popular roadkill feast dish served on short notice is *Smashlik*.

Smashlik

Skin, clean, and debone two pounds of kosher mystery meat (without cloven feet).

In a mixing bowl, prepare a marinade of ½ cup of olive oil, one large minced onion, the juice of one lemon, ½ teaspoon of salt, and ¼ teaspoon of pepper. Rub marinade into meat and let stand for six hours.

Preheat oven to 325 degrees.

Drain meat and reserve the marinade. Brown meat in a greased skillet, then place in a baking pan, baste with marinade, and bake for one hour or until tender.

Serve on a bed of rice and be sure to thank everyone for contributing to such a nice meal after the hard day you've had.

Kosher meats consumed by orthodox Jews must be drained of blood and consumed within a seventy-two hour period, which for a roadside shopper is more than enough time.

Saudi Arabia

One of the most popular Arabian dishes is called *Kharoof Mahshy* which translated is roast stuffed kid and any country that not only roasts but stuffs their kids should be avoided by all roadside shoppers. Except those traveling with unruly American kids.

Syria

Strategically vulnerable to the armies of shoppers driving over the land bridge linking Africa, Asia, and Europe, Syria's pastoral economy is flush with domesticated animals whose collective IQ matches that of an eggplant. Everywhere you go, a lamb is sure to be laid low. This baked lamb meat loaf is guaranteed to provide ninety-nine percent of the complete daily nutritional requirement for adults.

Kibbeh L'Bits

In a mixing bowl, cover 1 ½ cups of cracked wheat with cold water, let stand for ten minutes, then drain and press out the water. In another mixing bowl combine one pound of ground lamb, one large chopped onion, two teaspoons of salt, and ½ teaspoon of pepper. Add cracked wheat to meat mixture and neatly knead until well mixed.

In a skillet, sauté ¼ pound of ground lamb, one small minced onion, two tablespoons of pine nuts, and ½ teaspoon of cinnamon for five minutes.

Preheat oven to 350 degrees.

Take half of the cracked wheat and lamb mixture and press it into an ungreased baking dish. Spoon all of the sautéed lamb and onion mixture on top, then cover with remaining half of cracked wheat and lamb mixture. Cut a diamond pattern into the top of the meat loaf and pour two tablespoons of melted butter over all. Bake uncovered for forty minutes.

Serve hot or cold, as required.

Turkey

Instantbul, a capital dish, is easily had by sliding up against a ox-driven carriage and slicing off a hunk of haunch. If the cart is owned by a fundamentalist Turk with a big sword, you  will become a part of another popular dish, *Doner Kebabs*, named after the Donner Party of the Sierra Nevadas, another bunch of turkeys.

9

THE ROADKILL CUISINE OF ASIA AND INDIA

This wide, diverse region includes China, India, Japan, Korea, Mongolia, and if there is any gas left over, the mainland countries of Southeast Asia and island countries of the Malay Archipelago. Asia does not give up its roadside selections easy. The continent and subcontinents includes forbidding high desert, dense rain forest, and steep mountain terrain that even Sir Edmund Hillary ignored. Ignore the dangers and don't miss the opportunity to shop for exotic foods in equally exotic hopping carts.

Asia

Pakistan

East Pakistan was renamed Bangladesh in 1971 in hopes of avoiding the annual flooding and tropical cyclones from the Bay of Bengal. Low fat chance. Although finally  self-sufficient in rice, residents bang la' dish at every Red Cross meat rationing. In the Muslim formerly West Pakistan, the troublesome mujahidins have returned to Afghanistan and the roads are now clear for a popular Pakistani roadkill dish.

Chicken Peeloff

Peel, pluck, clean, and debone chicken. Cut one pound of the meat into cubes and toss the rest. Place the chicken in a mix-

ing bowl and add two large chopped onion, three cloves of minced garlic, one tablespoon of ground coriander, one teaspoon of salt, and ¾ teaspoon of pepper. Mix well and let stand for one hour.

In a skillet, sauté four cloves and one tablespoon of coriander seeds in one tablespoon of olive oil for one minute. Add meat mixture and sauté until meat turns opaque, then add 1½ cups of cooked rice, ¾ tablespoon of saffron dissolved in ¾ tablespoon of milk, and one cup of plain yogurt. Stir, cover, and cook on low heat for thirty minutes.

India

The Hindus don't eat beef and the Muslims don't eat pork so a good Lutheran can make his or her own *Delhi Sandwich* with a holy animal pressed between two rental cars. The Grand Truck Road from Lahore in the northeast all the way to Calcutta is the Indy 500 of hurry curry, a packed roadway where camels, cows, dogs, and other four-legged lunch boxes are served fresh.

One of the more unusual roadside taste treats in India is the mongoose, an otter-like snake eater often washed out of their burrows by flash floods.

Rikki-Sticki-Taffy

Clean, skin, and quarter one mongoose.

In a large pot, boil four cups of water. Add mongoose pieces to boiling water and boil for one hour, skimming frequently. Remove meat, drain, and let sit in a bowl of cold water for twenty-four hours. Remove and drain.

In a skillet, heat ¼ cup of olive oil. Roll meat in two beaten eggs, then two cups of bread crumbs, shaking off any excess. Fry in oil until golden brown.

Serve on puffed or sticky rice.

Nepal sits on the right shoulder of India and the ritual initiation dish served to seekers after enlightenment in the Himalayas is *Katfondue.* The spotted white feline filets are stored next to the yeti eggs in any lama's high mountain icebox.

A popular dish of East India, particularly among expatriate Brits, is a spicy mixture of peas, rice, and purebred roadkill.

Kedgeree of Pedigree

Soak two cups of dried split peas for two hours in cold water, then drain well.

In a skillet, melt two tablespoons of butter and sauté one large minced onion.

Add peas and cook well.

In a double boiler, mix the peas and onion with two cups of cooked rice, two cups of cooked, chopped roadkill pedigree,

¼ cup of butter, ¼ cup of cream, two tablespoons of chopped parsley leaves, and salt and pepper to taste. Warm thoroughly.

Serve with chopped hard-boiled eggs sprinkled on top of each serving.

Myanmar

When Burma was renamed Myanmar, one of the most famous American shaving cream companies went out of business and their roadside signs fell under the weight of their own pith. The prospects of roadkill in Myanmar are increasing with logging companies cutting new roads into the tropical rain forests in the high stakes race for teak and other exotic hardwoods. Once chain saws empty the treetops, a great previously unavailable variety of wildlife will be on the roadside market.

Mongolia

Roads in Mongolia are best described as tire tracks, perfect to keep the domesticated herds in steppe but tough on rental cars, escalating the cost per pound for good roadkill. The descendants of Genghis and Kubla Kahn have much more horsepower than your trusted steed so be safe and look for your Mongolian beef in the better Chinese restaurants. If you are on good behavior, the locals down at the corner yurt will offer boiled mutton and a tumbler of *airag*, fermented mare's milk, another good reason to keep moving.

China

There are five distinctly regional roadside cookeries in China; Peking or northern style, rated mild and often steamed; Mongolian barbeque, a buffet; Shanghai or eastern style, using seafood and lightly spiced rich sauces; Szechwan and Hunan style, full of garlic, chili peppers, and scallions to warm your day; and the less spicy Cantonese style. At Buck's Bass Resort in northernmost Minnesota, Buck's Chinese cook Sum Dim Wit mixes the styles in preparing the hors d'oerves for the happy hour in the Valhalla Lounge. A roadside shopper in China can take similar liberties with popular dishes.

Egg Soo Young

In a wok or skillet, heat two tablespoons of olive oil and stir-fry one minced slice of ginger root, six chopped green onions, two thinly sliced stalks of celery, and one cup of mystery meat. Cook thoroughly and remove.

In a mixing bowl, beat six eggs with one teaspoon of salt and ½ teaspoon of pepper. Add vegetable and meat mixture to eggs.

In a smaller skillet, heat one tablespoon of olive oil and spoon mixture into the skillet in small quantities. Fry golden brown on both sides.

A California version of this recipe is Egg Geo Young, which uses corporate nest eggs instead of the more common chicken eggs.

Chinese cooks use only small, fresh portions prepared quickly in oiled woks because in the not-so-distant past, refrigeration was non-existent. One Chinese mein dish involves the most popular canine export and a local ingredient that can be purchased with any shopping cart.

Chow Chow Mein

Clean, skin, and debone one chow chow. Cook meat in any fashion, then cut meat into two-inch strips, enough for four cups.

In a wok or skillet, stir-fry two thinly sliced stalks of celery, six chopped green onions, two seeded and julienned green peppers, two cups of sliced mushrooms, two cups of bean sprouts, and the meat for about six minutes. Add one chopped tomato and one cup of chow chow stock. Season with salt and pepper to taste.

Serve on a bed of fried noodles, or steamed rice for *Chopped Chow Chow Fuey Suey*. Garnish with slices of chilled, poached, blue-black tongue of this midsized muscular pedigree.

Taiwan

Main highways circle the island Republic of China and secondary roads carry shoppers into the mountainous interior which is also intersected by a centrally located cross island highway. The nature parks are a good place to start your shopping. If you have your own vehicle, it should be noted that even travel guides state that priority on the roads goes to the hungriest drivers. If you don't have your own shopping cart, express buses connect cities with major scenic (roadkill) spots. Few bus (or for that matter, taxi) drivers speak English so exact written roadside shopping instructions must be distributed before departure.

Korea

The Irish of Asia prefer to eat all their food courses at once, hanjongshik style. Any main dish is accompanied by rice, soup, kimchi, and several smaller side dishes. *Kimchi* is an internationally famous cabbage dish that is fermented in chili pepper sauce and the reason aficionados wear adult diapers under their street clothes.

Two familiar roadkill dishes are *Kalbi* and *Pulgogi*. *Kalbi* looks like spare ribs; the more popular *Pulgogi* is strips of either pork or preferably beef that have been marinated in garlic and other spices, then cooked over a charcoal fire. This Seoul food can be eaten during any meal period in South Korea. Above the demilitarized zone, the North Koreans only yearn to eat South Korea's lunch.

Japan

Smaller than California and with a largely uninhabitable volcanic mountain environment, Japanese urban centers are so jam packed with people that you must leave the cities to find anything loose. In the countryside, the English translations on the road signs disappear and it's important to be familiar with local customs. The exchange of the gift of roadkill builds personal relationships; if you ask a local Shinto priest to help clean a macaque monkey, offer them a share in the proceeds. If you've already skinned and quartered the monkey but need a bowl of rice to make it a full meal, remember that the wrapping of a roadkill morsel is as important as the contents and that monkey comes with its own decorative package.

Fish plays a very large role in the Japanese diet. *Sushiyuki* is the Japanese open-faced sandwich, with a slice of raw fish atop an oblong of vinegared rice. Accidentally flipped, the sandwich becomes *Yukisushi*. The red meat of choice is the famous Kobe beef, filets from coddled cattle that have been force fed premium beer and massaged by nude geisha girls until the meat reaches its legendary marbled excellence. Oh, to be a Kobe for a day.

The premier roadshop trophy on this island empire is Haiku Tsuro, the wild white crane that can be purchased with as small a vehicle as a city scooter. The Haiku Tsuro mates for life; be decent and make both birds lose face. Hit hard and fast.

Tora Tora Tempura

In a mixing bowl, combine two cups of flour, one teaspoon of salt, ¼ teaspoon of pepper, one tablespoon of melted butter, and two beaten egg yolks. Stir well and slowly mix in ¾ cup of flat Japanese beer (Sapporo comes in an attractive can). Cover and refrigerate batter for ten hours.

Pluck, clean, and cut two Haiku Tsuro breasts into ¼-inch strips. Slice one large eggplant into ¼-inch thick slices.

Dip eggplant and Haiku Tsuro strips into batter and deep-fry until golden brown.

Serve with soy sauce and wasabi.

Philippines

Jeepneys, brightly painted minibuses built on the frames of World War Two jeeps, are the recreational shopping carts of choice  for gathering ingredients of the Philippine national dish, *Adobo* (or *Adobong*). The great thing about *Adobo* is that it can be made with any kind or combination of meats.

Attaboy Adobong

Preheat oven to 350 degrees.

Skin, clean, and cut into cubes one pound of lean mystery meat (as pork-like as you can manage). Skin, clean, and quarter two pounds of fowl mystery meat (as chicken-like as you can manage).

In a Dutch oven, place meats along with one cup of water, ⅓ cup of white wine vinegar, three cloves of minced garlic, two tablespoons of soy sauce, one teaspoon of salt, and ½ teaspoon of black pepper. Cover and simmer for one hour, then remove meats.

In a skillet, heat two tablespoons of olive oil and brown meats. Reduce broth in a saucepan.

Serve by pouring sauce over meat on top of a bed of steamed rice.

Mabuhay!

Southeast Asia

Vietnam

Even though the Ho Chi Minh Trail has been resurfaced, the spartan North Vietnamese have long since given up road meals to live on C-rations left behind in the warehouses of Cam  Rhan Bay over twenty years ago. Most South Vietnamese have relocated to Minnesota or Montana; the remaining few send secret love notes to the French or star in Oliver Stone movies. In a country with a long history of internecine warfare, the ascribed national dish is *Sum Di Young*, a generic recipe using any local fauna. Visitors can take advantage of the fledgling tourist industry by renting a car and driver to shop National Highway One from Hanoi all the way to Ho Chi Minh City and the fertile Mekong Delta.

Laos

The road system of the landlocked high country of Laos is minimal and impassable during the monsoon season of April to September.  The subsistence farmers living in isolated villages along the valley floors are frugal, humorless, and watchful animal tenders. The capitol is Luang Prabang and the most popular open market roadkill dish is *Kung Pow Bing Bang*, an unrecognizable medley of flavors.

Thailand

Thai food has a reputation for being hot and spicy, particularly the coconut curries with the singe on top. A capital Thai recipe is *Bang-*  *cock*, a reckless, road-crossing version of drunken chicken. Restaurant menus are good guides to local cuisine and roadside shoppers will notice that many Thai dishes end with the word phrik, especially the restaurants along the three infamous side streets of Bangkok, Pat Pong I, II, and III. Which is a good enough reason to keep your foreign ambassador zipped up inside your embassy.

Bangkok is a traffic nightmare. In the confusion, a terrific shopping experience can be had by renting a cycloped or moped to ram through a crowded farmer's market and nab the makings for *Phried Phedal Phood*.

Phried Phedal Phood

In a wok or skillet, heat two tablespoons of olive oil and sauté three cloves of minced garlic until light brown. Add one pound of boneless chopped market meat (whatever is running slower than you) and lightly sauté. Add ¼ cup of red chili peppers, two tablespoons of sugar, and one tablespoon of fish sauce and stir-fry for three minutes.

Add ½ cup of shelled unsalted peanuts and stir-fry for one more minute.

Serve with steamed rice for three phriends.

Cambodia

Rice farmers in the flat delta rice fields use water buffalos for rice cultivation. Occasionally a farmer's daughter will borrow the beast to go shopping for the latest colors from  Khmer Rouge, the famous Cambodian cosmetics manufacturer. Collision damages from shopping the out-of-water buffalo far exceed insurance company limits. Unless you plan to turn your rental vehicle into a paddy wagon, pass Cambodia by.

Malay Archipelago

Borneo

South by southwest of the Philippines is Borneo, an island where missionaries make it harder to get a head. In the lowland rain forests, however, a tree animal wins by a nose; the proboscis monkey. If an occupied tree is hit hard enough, it's possible to create a meal that is nothing to sneeze at.

Pabang Proboscis

Clean one monkey nose, trim off all fat and boogers, and soak overnight in cold salted water. Remove nose and rinse well in cold water. Place nose in a large pot with enough water to cover and add one chopped carrot, one large chopped onion, ½ slice lemon, one bay leaf, four cloves, one tablespoon salt, and ½ teaspoon of black pepper. Bring to a boil, then simmer uncovered for one hour. Remove nose, skin, return to broth with one cup of fish sauce (any commercial brand), and simmer for thirty minutes.

Serve with either plantain or red bananas.

Malaysia

Kuala Lumpur, the capital and largest city, has a sizable Australian expatriate population which has created a need for illegal food  imports to keep the blokes in both familiar and forbidden homeland foodstuffs. Secret culinary societies sponsor annual banquets where the host tries to outdo the previous sponsor. *Koala Tempur* is a staple at the Australian Retired Tourism Officials Association banquet.

Indonesia

With over 17,000 islands, the world's largest archipelago is distinguished with two principal regional cuisines, Java and West Sumatra.  Javalinos like their roadkill sweet but spicy; the Sumatras, led by Frank and Nancy, prefer it pepper hot.

A popular dish most everywhere is fried rice and skewed, grilled meat dipped in soy or peanut sauce called *Nasti Goring*. Somewhere on these islands there must be some nasti meat that can be gored, skewed, and grilled.

10

THE ROADKILL CUISINE OF OCEANIA

Islands have a geological history of being part of larger land masses and, once the break was made, island animals were left stranded to evolve with a local twist. How they evolved was first altered by the arrival of the white he-devil and his idiot domestics like dogs, cats, and pigs. If that wasn't bad enough, the new men on the block imported additional non-native animals for food and sport, which pushed the original populations into even less undesirable habitat. Famous small island groupings such as the Galapagos offer up exotic roadkill potential but their habitation and road system is so sparse that traffic incidents occur only when the cruise ships drop the gang planks. But that doesn't mean all islands are a poor investment in time and energy.

Australia

Australia is a roadside shoppers dream. This large island with the fourth largest wilderness in the world is packed with animals, large and  small. Do you want horse meat? No problem, mate! There are over 200,000 feral horses or brombay running loose over the outback. Did you miss a chance on a North African camel? No problem, mate! Feral camels are just speed humps in the Australian outback. Small animals? Once introduced for sport hunting and food in the mid-1800s, rabbits are now so numerous that you can do two- and three-fers. Cane toads? Another import mistake. But there are better eating morsels. Animals with valuable skins? Sure. Enough red fox to even cover the less valuable hide of your mother-in-law. Animals that remind you of your noisy back fence? There are over twelve million feral cats; multiplied by nine lives gives you one hundred eight million soul-crunching opportunities. National symbols like koala bears? Maybe, if you have a vehicle that can climb a tree. Doesn't mean you can't try and get a good run on a tree that slopes. You might shake the sleepy marsupial out of its perch.

Food or tucker for city folks reflects the habits and palettes of the colonializing English but natives still prefer caterpillars and iguanas, which adequately explains English food. Favored bush tucker for Aboriginal children and women is witchetty grubs, fat white larvae eaten raw or rolled in ash. Aboriginal men are found outback eating water buffalo steaks smoked over bamksia cones, which adequately explains the true natural order.

Aussies are thought to subsist on "floaters chased with a tinnie or stubbie of the amber fluid", or an English meat pie backstroking across a plate of soupy peas and gravy plus a beer. That's not exactly true. More often it's two tinnies of the amber fluid.

The meat diet of the Australians reflects the diversity of available road food. Rabbit meat mixed in bread dough is baked as a breakfast dish. The big-footed macropod, the kangaroo or roo, is served in restaurants. The sweet game meat of kangaroos and the wannabee wallabee can be smoked or thrown on the barbie. Jackeroos and Jillaroos have equal opportunity to serve in this country and roadside shoppers may have to speed up to thirty miles an hour for a short distance to get a jump on a good piece of Australian tail.

Tail O' Roo

Preheat oven to 350 degrees.

Skin, clean, and cut into chunks one kangaroo tail.

In a large skillet, melt ¼ cup of butter and brown tail. Add three cups of beef or chicken stock, one teaspoon of salt, and ½ teaspoon of pepper. Bring to a boil, then transfer to a large casserole dish, cover, and bake for four hours. Add one large chopped onion, one large chopped carrot, three large chopped celery stalks, and one large chopped rutabaga. Cover and bake for another hour. Drain off liquid, thicken with two tablespoons of flour, and add back to meat and vegetables.

Serve with boiled potatoes and a couple of tubes of Fosters.

Joey ain't gonna jump no more no more.

New Zealand

South east of Australia, New Zealanders or kiwis live on two main islands, North and South. The rugged countryside is dominated by snowcapped mountains and most live on the more temperate north island. Dairy farming and commercial sheep ranching provide for domesticated herd shopping and a favorite New Zealander dish is *Colonial Goose*, a boned leg of mutton stuffed with foreskins. New Zealand is actually the world's largest exporter of lamb and not coincidentally a very important supplier of lamb foreskins for the British condom industry. The native Maori have assimilated many of the British food habits, but resist the transparent population control efforts. Unless the Brits are in a missionary position.

Other Islands

Micronesia

This consists of a group of islands located in the west Pacific Ocean and includes the isles of Langersham, several pancreas-shaped masses primarily known for their manufacture of sugar products. Melanesia includes the islands closest to Australia and are inhabitated by the Melanoma family, relatives of the darker-skinned Australian aborigines. The off-road cuisine found on the island group called Microwavia are best known for their quick and easy preparation. All the small islands in Oceania require complicated and expensive travel arrangements, inflating the cost per pound ratio out of reach for most shoppers. The most famous island in Polynesia is the Isle of Gilligan, at first uncharted but discovered in the backwaters of CBS with an exotic, erotic cuisine that carries with it complaints of too little ginger. For any hungry roadside shopper, it's best to concentrate on the carnage cornucopia called Australia.

Tahiti

Tahiti, Moorea, Raiatea, Bora Bora, and other islands in the Society Islands group are full of free-ranging animals that seem to share a common ownership. Chickens, black pigs, and red dogs are fair game on the macadam roads that follow the shorelines of these islands. Fowl feeding on mangoes and papayas self-marinade their sweet meats for the serious shopper. As in any paradise, there is one small catch: the small islands won't have any vehicles for rent outside of mopeds, and a good-size pig in a bad mood can do more damage to the cycle and rider than the cycle and rider can do to the pig. Choose your target carefully.

Tasmania

The Tasmanian Devil, a carrion-eating marsupial, cleans the roads of Tasmania, an island off the southeast Australian coastline and home of a terrible prison colony. The little devil deserves an exclusive.

New Guinea

The second largest island in the world is covered with tropical rain forest and exotic wildlife. Unfortunately the rudimentary road system and northern snowcapped mountains allows little access to the limited edition marsupials. Possums can be found elsewhere, even at home.

Extra Special Bonus

Since we're this far south . . .

Antarctica

The ice cap of the South Pole is host to many ecotourists in heated tracked vehicles wildly careening through penguin populations. Now cruelly dependent on Twinkies and other nutritious American/Euro-trash snack cakes, the large Emperor and smaller Adelie penguins risk their lives at the crowded photo opportunity sites. Elephant seals are the only other mammal within reach along the scarcely inhabited coastline but they are too cautious to be a predictable food source. At the North Pole there is at least a small chance to run over a sleeping polar bear with a mute dog sled team. The interior of Antarctica is so empty of foodstuffs that once the last tourist ship pulls from the dock, the chefs of the nearby eighteen nation research stations send out kitchen stewards to chip any squashed penguins out of the frozen mush.

Penguin in Ice Pick

Clean and remove the tuxedo from one Emperor penguin.

In a large pot, boil five cups of water, three chopped celery stalks, one medium chopped onion, ¼ cup of chopped parsley leaves, three tablespoons of lemon juice, one teaspoon of salt, and ½ teaspoon of pepper. Reduce to simmer and cook penguin in pot for one hour or until tender. Remove penguin and set aside. Strain the stock, return to heat, and add two tablespoons of gelatin dissolved in ¼ cup of chicken stock, two tablespoons of capers, three tablespoons of lemon juice, and salt and pepper to taste.

Chill stock until it begins thickening. Chop cooked penguin meat. In a chilled gelatin mold, pour a layer of the stock (now aspic), then place a layer of the meat, then aspic, then meat, ending with aspic. Chill until firm.

Dip mold in warm water, loosen aspic with an ice pick, and shake firmly out of mold on to a bed of iceberg lettuce.

Serve with a dollop of mayonnaise and utter disregard.

This recipe can be used with the Gentoo, Chinstrap, Macroni, and Rockhopper Penguins as well.

Afterword

The impulse to return home after an adventurous and nutritious trip abroad may be a simple intuition that your domestic state-side life needs tending or a strong physical message that you are just too full to continue on, even for the smallest roadkill snack.

At that point, Buck recommends that you fold camp and selectively gather the mementos of your distended gourmet holiday. CAUTION: Many of your overseas roadside purchases came in decorative wrappers that cannot be brought home. Other body parts such as Dumbo dentures are not even allowed to leave the country of origin, unless they are carved into aged piano keys. You may be left with only the memories of an international moveable feast to carry you through the leaner months ahead, which should be enough if you did it right. Burp!

TEN SPEED PRESS
P. O. Box 7123
Berkeley, California 94707